50 Film Ideas
You Really
Need to Know
Helen O'Hara

greenfinch

Contents

Introduction 3

THE INVENTION OF CINEMA
01 Early moving images 4
02 Early projection 8
03 Feature length 12
04 Colour 16

FILM BASICS
05 Montage and editing 20
06 The close-up 24
07 Cinematography 28
08 Mise-en-scène 32
09 Sound and soundtrack 36
10 Special effects 40
11 Visual effects 44
12 Film formats and
    aspect ratios 48
13 Frame rates 52
14 The movie star 56
15 Animation 60
16 Documentary 64
17 Distribution 68

MAJOR HOLLYWOOD ERAS
18 The silent era 72
19 The studio era 76
20 The Production Code 80
21 The New Hollywood 84
22 High concept 88
23 The indie era 92
24 Film franchises 96
25 #MeToo 100

WORLD MOVEMENTS
26 German Expressionism 104
27 Surrealism 108
28 Italian neorealism 112
29 French New Wave 116
30 Japanese golden age 120
31 Martial arts movies 124
32 Indian film 128
33 Third Cinema 132
34 New Mexican cinema 136
35 Nigerian film 140
36 Dogme 95 144

FILM THEORY
37 The auteur theory 148
38 Marxist film theory 152
39 The gaze theory 156
40 Queer theory 160
41 Structuralist and
    linguistic film theory 164
42 Postmodernism 168

GENRE
43 The Western 172
44 Horror 176
45 Film noir 180
46 The musical 184
47 The action movie 188
48 Comedy 192
49 Propaganda films 196
50 Science fiction and fantasy 200

Glossary 204
Index 206

Introduction

Film critic Roger Ebert:
'The movies are like a machine that generates empathy.'

Humans have been fascinated by shadows dancing on walls for millennia, but it was not until the end of the 19th century that photography and projection reached the point at which filmmakers could control those shadows and shape them into endless forms and stories. In the last 130 years, cinema has spread across the globe, enabling audiences to watch impossible things and share a profound art experience.

For such a young art form, cinema's development has been rapid and full of incident. You might call it colourful, except that developing colour took a little time at the very beginning. But already, philosophies have been attempted and abandoned, theories applied or discredited, and ways of working adopted and codified.

To me, it seems impossible to boil the entirety of film down to just 50 ideas. Instead I have provided what I believe to be a useful cross-section of, and introduction to, film practice, history and theory. This effort may therefore be less conceptual than some books in this series, but film has been shaped more by practical than theoretical forces and it felt important to acknowledge that, discussing Hollywood studios alongside structuralism. I have covered other influential international film movements, though again, this cannot be comprehensive: Chinese film alone would require multiple books.

Hopefully this book will give you a starting point to decide what you would like to read more about, and certainly a few films to add to your watch list. More than anything, I hope it will remind you of the power and influence of cinema. We talk about the film industry, but it is also an art that has the potential to bring us together and to teach us new things about the world. For that reason it is important to protect and celebrate the films that move us, and the cinema itself.

Helen O'Hara

01 Early moving images

Humanity has been progressing towards moving images since the very start. A painting in the Karampuang cave in South Sulawesi, Indonesia, dates back over 50,000 years and shows a pig and three humans, presumably on a hunting expedition. Other figurative art around the world, from India to Lascaux, in France, shows action scenes of animals and people, often with a sense of movement and an apparent attempt to depict sequential actions. In the flickering light of a fire, they might have seemed to move and were perhaps used to narrate great exploits of hunting or survival.

Shadows around a campfire, however, leave no trace, and the first good evidence we have of actual moving images used for storytelling dates back to around 1420, when an Italian engineer called Giovanni Fontana published a reference to a 'magic lantern', which projected a cutout image of a devil against a wall in a larger form as part of a performance. These magic lanterns became more and more sophisticated through the centuries as scientific knowledge advanced. In 1797, Belgian scientist Étienne-Gaspard Robert established his own theatre in Paris and employed them in sophisticated ways, using a track to move the lantern backward or forward to change an image's size to eerie effect, often in support of actors telling a story onstage. The fact that Robert held regular lectures explaining his work does not appear to have detracted from their effect.

The illusion of movement

Moving images became more sophisticated in the 1800s after Peter Roget published his 1824 paper with the British Royal Society on 'The Persistence of Vision with Regard to Moving Objects'. This discussed the phenomenon whereby the retina retains an image for a fraction of a second after it has disappeared, so that if you show similar images quickly and in sequence, you can create the illusion of movement from one to the next. This inspired wild experimentation. The following year, Englishman John Ayrton Paris created the 'thaumatrope', a spinning disc with different pictures on each side that appeared to merge when the disc was spun around (the most famous shows a bird and a cage). A few years later, in 1831, the Belgian Joseph

Plateau created the 'phenakistoscope', a disc that spun like a record, causing near-identical images around its circumference to appear to move. They showed, for example, a woman beating her husband, or a man peddling a bike.

The best known of these spinning devices is the 'zoetrope'. Interestingly, historian Joseph Needham describes similar devices in China dating back to the Han dynasty in the 1000s, though it is not clear how much these succeeded in giving the illusion of movement. There is no evidence that English mathematician William George Horner knew about them in 1833, however, when he built a zoetrope (that name came from a later patent filed by American William F Lincoln in 1860). Once again these sport near-repeating images, but this time they are placed around the inside of a low, wide cylinder with narrow slots cut in the sides. By looking through these slots, several people at once can see galloping horses or jumping figures inside the disc as it spins.

The praxinoscope

The first person ever to run a strip of film in front of a projector seems to have been Frenchman Charles-Émile Reynaud. In 1877 he patented a new device called a 'praxinoscope', initially a sort of glorified zoetrope that used fixed mirrors in the centre of the cylinder to reflect the moving image. By 1879 he had refined it further, hiding his mechanism in a box with a screen in the front to provide a mini theatrical experience. He developed the Théâtre Optique in 1888. Projecting images for a group of people, on a much bigger screen and from a roll of pictures, this allowed him to show more elaborate scenes. By 1892 Reynaud was advertising Pantomimes Lumineuses shows at the Musée Grévin in Paris, using the device to tell longer stories to larger audiences. However, his system was soon eclipsed by the Lumière brothers' cinematographe, and Reynaud could no longer make his invention pay. He was, however, responsible for a key innovation: film perforations to move the roll at a uniform rate.

Capturing movement on camera

All of these devices used drawings rather than cameras for their input, however. It was a little later, in the 19th century, that pioneers attempting to study movement invented ways to record sequences of images at high speed. One such was Englishman Eadweard Muybridge, an extremely eccentric character who suffered serious head injuries in a stagecoach crash; shot and killed his wife's lover (though he was acquitted); and travelled widely to study photography all over the world. From 1878 onwards he took advantage of the increased sensitivity of photographic emulsion, which allowed near instantaneous photography for the first time, to begin a series of studies on animal locomotion. He contrived a number of cameras to photograph a galloping horse and show how it moved in motion (the general feeling was that it was less graceful than expected). He was so successful in capturing a sequence of images that his prints could be projected one after another to give the appearance of movement.

The kinetoscope

Thomas Edison is widely remembered as one of the greatest inventors ever to live, not least because he was also one of the greatest self-promoters in history. He displayed a 'kinetograph' motion-picture camera and a 'kinetoscope' peep-hole viewer to watch the resulting films in 1891, and sold thousands of the former in the United States and Europe, popularizing the concept of moving images. When cinema took off, Edison became a major supplier of cameras and film, and a significant voice for copyright and patent protection in the United States. However, while US sources sometimes credit Edison with the invention of cinema, it's fairer to say that he was part of the rush to the screen and not the sole man responsible. His kinetoscope only accomodated one viewer at a time.

Muybridge's process was developed further by Frenchman Étienne-Jules Marey, a groundbreaking cardiologist who was also chiefly interested in studying movement. In 1882 he created a 'chronophotographic gun' that could take 12 images per second. He struggled to play his images back initially, but a visit from Thomas Edison in 1889 helped him to solve that problem when they came up with a sprocketed mechanism to advance the film. However, Marey, like Muybridge before him, saw these sequences of film more as a scientific tool than an important technology in their own right, and made no attempt to use this new power to film material for a wider audience. British inventor William Friese-Greene, in the same year, patented his own motion-picture camera using paper and celluloid film; he sent details of his work to Thomas Edison, who started his lab working on the same problem and came up with the 'kinetoscope'. However, Friese-Greene never projected his work. That would require the involvement of the Lumière brothers. Nevertheless, all of the steps taken in the 19th century laid the foundations for the Lumières' work, and it was only by inventors sharing their discoveries and discussing their processes that cinema finally came about.

The condensed idea
From cave paintings to the projected image

02 Early projection

Many inventors in the late 19th century were working towards cinema, but its invention is generally credited to brothers Auguste and Louis Lumière, who first put all the elements together and projected their work publicly. Arguably the pair were born for the camera – their parents owned and ran a photographic portrait studio in the eastern French town where they grew up. They were technically minded from an early age, with Louis inventing a new 'dry plate' process to develop film while still a teenager. This innovation led to their father opening a factory in the suburbs of Lyon in 1881 to exploit the development that, 13 years later, was producing 15 million photographic plates a year.

The birth of the big screen

The two Lumière boys, however, had turned their attention (and their money) to the question of moving images. They bought the rights to a *cinématographe* machine created by inventor Léon Bouly after Bouly ran into financial trouble and could not afford his patent fees. His device had a key advantage over those of his competitors, including Edison's kinetograph: it could both record and project images. The pair tweaked and improved on Bouly's work and received their own patent in February 1895. Later that year, they gave their first commercial showings of projected film.

These included such scintillating subjects as workers leaving a factory, photographers disembarking from a riverboat and a baby eating a meal (Auguste's daughter, in fact). Despite such mundane activities, the mere prospect of seeing everyday life on a big screen was a draw and the new technology became a sensation, even if stories of people running in terror at *Arrival of a Train at La Ciotat* (1896) are mostly myths. Fellow industrialists and inventors, such as Léon Gaumont, attended the demonstrations and left fired up and ready to exploit this new medium; Gaumont's secretary Alice Guy would soon make what is thought to be the world's first narrative film, *The Cabbage Fairy* (1896), while Georges Méliès quickly pushed the boundaries of what film storytelling could do with his extravagant onscreen fantasies. The Lumière brothers themselves took their show on the road, visiting Bombay, London, New York City, Palestine, Cairo and Buenos Aires in the following year or so. But while they shot and exhibited globally, and sent out agents with cameras to capture footage of significant places and events, they were never particularly convinced of cinema's value themselves, and preferred to focus on the technological side than on the filmmaking opportunities.

Others saw more potential, however. Cinema spread internationally with astonishing speed, fuelled by urbanization and a growth in levels of disposable income that came alongside industrialization. Within ten years, cinema had established itself across the United States and was a major source of entertainment. By the 1930s, it would be America's leading export, and a major industry in Russia, the United Kingdom, Germany and India, to name but a few.

The first cinemas

Initially, film projection was a travelling feast. Without purpose-built movie houses, distributors literally travelled from town to town with a projector and a sheet to put on their shows. The very luckiest, in the big cities, might secure a cellar or warehouse floor for the event, but such precarious locations were a huge fire risk, especially given the highly flammable stocks of celluloid film. Some projectionists would share space and evening programmes with vaudeville acts, so that vaudeville's slight air of disreputability rubbed off on the new medium.

A cottage industry

At this time, the costs involved in filmmaking were not insurmountable. Independent filmmakers, such as female filmmakers Alice Guy and Lois Weber and Black filmmaker Oscar Micheaux, were able to establish their own film studios in what were essentially warehouse spaces with large windows, and to profitably make and release films from that base. It was only as films became longer and more expensive that larger studios crowded out these independent filmmakers.

Film piracy is a crime

In the early days of the film industry, it was common for film companies to create duplicates of one another's projects and sell them alongside their own. Thomas Edison finally took action against this, despite his own company also having engaged in the practice. He registered each frame of one of his films for copyright, before suing Pennsylvania-based producer Siegmund Lubin for copyright infringement. A district court initially decreed that film could not benefit from copyright law, but in April 1903 the Third Circuit Court of Appeals ruled that it could be copyrighted. Defiantly, Lubin kept going and was sued by Biograph that August for the same offence. It wasn't until the Townsend Amendment to the Copyright Act of 1909 came into force in 1912 that filmmakers got serious protection for their work.

The filming of subjects like boxing matches – projected to mixed audiences even though women were not allowed to attend live events – further threatened the good name of the nascent art form (not yet acknowledged as such). To combat this, many independent distributors began to emphasize their family values in order to attract women and children to shows and avoid the seedier elements. They advertised the educational and morally uplifting qualities of the films they planned to show and placed women in the box office and on the accompanying musical instruments to create a safe space for mixed audiences (and probably also to entice male viewers).

By 1905, purpose-built cinemas were springing up in towns and cities all over the Western world; by the outbreak of World War I, virtually every town would have one and larger cities had venues that resembled theatres. A seemingly insatiable appetite for fresh films developed, and theatre owners would put together new programmes of films regularly: sometimes setting a theme for an evening, or providing live music, commentary or other performances alongside the film. As films grew longer, however, many of these additional elements were dropped, leaving just music accompanying the images onscreen.

With the war came an abrupt break in production in most European countries – something that the US industry used decisively to pull far ahead of its rivals. However, film remained a popular escape from stories of the battlefield, and the medium continued its exponential growth through the war and after. Annual production of film in the United States, for example, leapt from 38,000 feet in 1897 to 20 million feet by 1920. By the 1930s, almost everyone in the Western world went to the cinema, most of them weekly, and billions of tickets were sold annually. The money involved grew to such a level that cinema itself became industrialized under the studio system, amping up production to meet apparently limitless demand. Even by 20th-century standards, it was a dizzyingly fast rise to prominence for an entire industry.

The condensed idea
An industry is born

03 Feature length

For the purposes of general distribution and award consideration, a 'feature' film is now considered to refer to anything longer than 60 minutes, though it is rare to find a feature that short. Most Western films are between 85 and 185 minutes, with the vast majority clustered between 90 and 120 minutes. But it was never inevitable that this would become the standard.

Initially, films were only seconds long; the moving image was the draw, not so much the subject depicted. The somewhat mundane Lumière brothers' *Workers Leaving the Lumière Factory* (1895) offered scenes of everyday life lasting under a minute, for example. However, filmmakers wanted more freedom to work on longer forms. A key innovation that allowed them to do so was the Latham loop, a device

Bollywood

From their very early days, Bollywood films have characteristically had long average run times, with two-and-a-half to three-hour films as the norm. Some, such as 2001's hugely successful colonialist cricket drama *Lagaan*, are even longer, at 3 hours 44 minutes. This is partly due to the frequent inclusion of song-and-dance sequences that might add up to half an hour of a film's run time. From an exhibitor's point of view this creates opportunities for selling food during intermissions. But it's also felt that longer films allow more complex storytelling and multiple subplots, therefore creating more chances to engage everyone's attention (why choose between action and romance when you can have both?) This last point seems to be key for Bollywood filmmakers: they have more time to lay out their hero's motivations and the challenges they face, to deliver twists and turns, and to build satisfying emotional pay-offs for everyone involved.

that created a small loop of slack film just before the camera's gate and that absorbed strain on the film (which was greater with longer films) as it passed through the camera. The device prevented longer film strips from breaking and proved foundational to all film projection from this time on.

Quickly filmmakers' ambitions grew. The earliest long-form films were essentially sports broadcasts. The *Corbett-Fitzsimmons Fight* (1897) was a 100-minute long, specially staged boxing match, and a startling feat for the time. The director was Enoch J Rector, who shot the film on widescreen on 63mm nitrate film over 11,000 feet of stock. He used three adjacent cameras, even filming the lulls between rounds and the crowd storming the ring at the end of the fight. It democratized the sport because women were generally not allowed to watch boxing live, but could watch films about it, as could everyone in states where the sport was banned.

Fictional filmmakers also raised their ambitions, though at considerably greater expense and effort, since telling their stories often involved multiple sets, actors, costumes and scene changes. By 1904 Georges Méliès had made the extravagant, 20-minute-long *The Impossible Voyage*, with its iconic ship-landing-in-the-moon's-eye shot, and in 1906 Alice Guy made *The Life of Christ*, a comparative epic at 33 minutes long.

The first feature-length films

The first dramatic film at what is now considered 'feature' length was Charles Tait's *The Story of the Kelly Gang* (1906), from Australia. It tells the story of Ned Kelly, a 'bushranger', or outlaw, who had a brief but notorious stand-off with police some 26 years earlier. The film took six months to make but proved an enormous hit, recouping its budget during its initial week of trial screenings in country towns. It filled Melbourne cinemas for five weeks straight, with live performers providing sound effects, and toured for more than 20 years. It was instant evidence of something that Tait and his co-producer brothers, all of whom had a background on the stage, had suspected: that popular theatrical hits could also work as films.

That said, it took a little while for the word to get around. Early distribution tended to dub one film a 'feature' and then build a programme of shorter films and newsreels around it. So, one 20- or

30-minute 'two-reeler' might anchor a longer programme of entertainment, along with live music from an organ or violin. A 'nickelodeon' might charge five cents (a nickel) and allow spectators to stay as long as they liked, but the more expensive, permanent cinemas wanted more expensive product to run. These 'first run' cinemas might charge as much as $1.50 for entry, and with that higher price came high expectations. Theatre owners found that longer films, with stories akin to theatre and established star names, enabled them not only to charge higher prices, but also to make higher profits.

Pushing the limits

By the early 1910s, every filmmaking country was making what we would now consider feature films as the showcase element of their programming, and audiences continued to expand their attention spans. In 1915, D W Griffith had an enormous hit with his wildly racist blockbuster *The Birth of a Nation*, which played over 12 reels and lasted between 133 and 193 minutes, depending on projection speed (not yet standardized). It remains one of the highest-grossing films ever made, if adjusted for inflation.

Oscar winners

While the length of an average film in 2023 was 107 minutes, the average Best Picture winner at the Academy Awards is considerably longer, at 138 minutes. This includes the nearly four-hour likes of *Gone with the Wind* (1939), *Ben-Hur* (1959), *Lawrence of Arabia* (1962) and *The Lord of the Rings: The Return of the King* (2003). The average length of a nominee in this category is also well north of the average, suggesting that longer pictures have a better chance at the Oscars. Interestingly, this is also true of very high-grossing films: adjusting for inflation, only *E.T. the Extra-Terrestrial* (1982) in the top 10 highest-grossing films ever comes in under two hours – and then only by six minutes.

Through the studio era of the 1930s, most films came in around the 90-minute mark, with film lengths swelling slightly upwards to an average of around 100 minutes by the 1950s. There were exceptions, of course: the landmark *Gone with the Wind* (1939) was 221 minutes long, or 238 minutes if you sat around for the overture, entr'acte and exit music. Alfred Hitchcock is reputed to have said that, 'The length of a film should be directly related to the endurance of a human bladder,' and that's about where most films end up, though average film lengths dropped slightly in the early VHS-era of the 1980s, the better to fit on one tape. Lengthier films like *Gone with the Wind*, *Lawrence of Arabia* (1962) and, more recently, Quentin Tarantino's *The Hateful Eight* (2015) and Brady Corbet's *The Brutalist* (2025), may come with intermissions for toilet breaks or – more importantly from the point of view of a cinema's profit margin – to buy more snacks.

The condensed idea
Long enough to tell a good story

04 Colour

Experiments in colour began almost as soon as film did. Early film was photosensitive enough to react to light and dark in an instant, and flexible enough to run through a camera at speed, but it could not yet marry these traits with sufficient chemical sensitivity to also reproduce colour. It would take some time until colour film became a viable option for most films, and even longer before filmmakers decided it could offer as much flexibility and expressiveness as black-and-white.

As a result, many of the early colour films were hand-tinted with dye on monochromatic photographic images. Sometimes the entire image would be tinted – blue washes were often used to indicate a nighttime setting, for example – but more elaborate processes saw colour applied selectively, with stencils employed to ensure consistency across a reel. Edison's *Annabelle Serpentine Dance* is a colour film dating back to 1895, when it was originally shown in his peepshow kinetoscope device, and depicts a dancer's skirts miraculously changing colour as she moves. By 1905, Pathé Frères' 44-minute *The Life and Passion of Jesus Christ* had been extensively colourized by a 100-person-strong unit.

Edward Raymond Turner patented a three-colour filter process in 1899, which used three rotating, coloured filters to create three images that, when placed together, would show full colour. This was not suitable for shooting rapid movement, but pointed to the way ahead. Turner died suddenly in 1903, but his process was developed into Kinemacolor in 1909, the first successful motion-picture colour process. This was an 'additive' colour process, using green and red filters to create its hues. This required a camera and projection speed of 32fps, 16 frames of each filter, but did not fully replicate the entire colour spectrum.

The arrival of Technicolor

The first Technicolor system, in 1916, worked the same way, but their Process 2, in 1922, pioneered another approach. This 'subtractive' method used a 'beam-splitter' to simultaneously expose two consecutive frames, one with a red filter and one with green. The two frames were then toned and cemented together to create a colour image of a type used in 1925's *The Phantom of the Opera* and *Ben Hur*, for example. It worked, but proved tricky to use and the film was susceptible to 'bowing' from the heat of the projector. Process 3 was more streamlined but uptake was slow, and the arrival of the Great Depression meant that most studios rejected the additional expense of colour film. Process 4, however, was another matter. It used a three-strip process with a beam-splitter but also a split prism, creating three-colour-matrix films covering separate parts of the spectrum, each loaded with the appropriate dye and brought into contact with a clear black-and-white film (with the soundtrack and frame lines pre-printed). The result was a fully colour film strip. Disney was an early adopter, for 1932's *Silly Symphony* movie *Flowers and Trees*. By 1935 live-action features such as *Becky Sharp* were shot fully in colour.

The process was still tricky, requiring much brighter studio lights and a colour supervisor from Technicolor to oversee the sets and costumes. In 1941, the company introduced its single-strip Monopack film for location shooting, but this had a more obvious grain than the

Jack Cardiff

Cinematographer and director Jack Cardiff worked with some of the greatest directors of all time, including Alfred Hitchcock, John Huston and King Vidor. However, it was his three films with Michael Powell and Emeric Pressburger that made his name and demonstrated the full artistic potential of colour film. The saturated colours of *Black Narcissus* (1947) and *The Red Shoes* (1948) drew gasps from contemporary audiences and have inspired filmmakers such as Martin Scorsese ever since. Prefiguring the work of subsequent colour enthusiasts from Russell Metty (*All That Heaven Allows*; 1955) and Christopher Doyle (*In The Mood For Love*; 2000), Cardiff showed that colour can be used expressionistically rather than be tied to reality as Truffaut feared.

three-strip original, which remained dominant. Still, Technicolor more or less *was* colour in Hollywood until two blows hit its model: an antitrust ruling in 1947 that demanded the company make its equipment available outside the big studios, and the arrival of Eastmancolor in 1950. This was an economical, single-strip negative process that effectively made Technicolor's three-strip process obsolete, as well as being compatible with the widescreen likes of CinemaScope that arrived soon after.

Colour scepticism

It is worth noting that not everyone in Hollywood embraced colour. As late as 1966, Andrei Tarkovsky called it 'a commercial gimmick'. Monochrome remained the norm for many years, and not only for budgetary reasons. It was not until 1957 that the majority of films worldwide were made in colour, and some genres were slower to adopt it than others. Westerns were more likely to be in colour than war films for nearly two decades. While the likes of Walt Disney and Alfred Hitchcock were colour fans, many directors were sceptical or downright hostile, and until well into the 1970s monochrome was considered more aesthetically pure by many, with colour a mere commercial necessity. François Truffaut considered colour damaging

The digital intermediate

When film, or digitally shot images, are transferred to digital, the 'digital intermediate' (DI) print, can be tweaked and altered. This is where computer VFX may be added, but also where a cinematographer can go in and colour-correct or colour grade the film, altering its tone. A film may be desaturated or tinted, enhancing its setting or mood. That is how we got the sepia tones of *O Brother, Where Art Thou?* (2000), one of the first films where the entire digital intermediate was colour graded (in that case by cinematographer Roger Deakins), or the monochrome segments of *Pleasantville* (1998), which was originally shot entirely in colour. It is now entirely standard to alter the image in the DI.

and overly realistic. Other directors have chosen black-and-white over colour even into the modern day, with filmmakers from John Ford to the Coen Brothers opting for monochrome even when colour was an option; this often signifies a period setting (in films such as *Oppenheimer* (2023) or *Schindler's List* (1993)). Some use it part of the time for effect, so we get the sepia tones of the Kansas scenes of *The Wizard of Oz* (1939) to heighten the contrast with the Technicolor Oz, or the coloured real world of *A Matter of Life and Death* (1946) with the monochrome heaven.

By the late 1990s, digital video had reached a point where it could displace film – especially since, around the same time, the impermanence of the Eastmancolor process, in particular, was becoming apparent. Colour films of the 1950s began to fade badly and the long process of restoration and preservation began. George Lucas shot *Star Wars: Attack of the Clones* on high-definition digital video in 2002, helping to popularize that new medium. While there were initially concerns that digital video was less sensitive to low light conditions, improving camera sensitivity during the 2000s steadily diminished those concerns. Far more extensive colour grading and colour correction using the digital intermediate arguably allowed colour to be used more expressively than ever, so that studios can now change their films to monochrome after shooting in colour (*Logan* (2017) and *Godzilla Minus One* (2023) both had black-and-white versions made) and use colour as artistically as Truffaut could ever have wished.

The condensed idea
The choice of colour can shape a film's mood

05 Montage and editing

Montage and editing, the placement and arrangement of images, is foundational to film. In fact, it is arguably the single, key element that distinguishes film from other art forms. Almost all films with a narrative – whether fictional, documentary or even surrealistic – construct that narrative by juxtaposing images and scenes, sometimes side by side in a split screen, but more often in sequence. Film stories are created in the edit, and much of the emotion of a film carried by the pace of editing and the selection of shots.

Montage has no precise corollary in any other art form. It is more granular and specific than scene changes in theatre; far faster moving than an equivalent descriptive passage in literature (a picture, after all, being worth a thousand words) or a musical progression. The precision of shot choice and ordering in good editing is probably closer to poetry than anything else. But editing was not always intrinsic to film; the first films were single shots with a camera locked

Soviet montage theory

The art of the montage was pushed forward hugely in the early 20th century by Russian filmmakers, particularly Sergei Eisenstein. See, for example, the famous Odessa Steps sequence in *Battleship Potemkin* (1925). Eisenstein's view was that a sequence of images was understood 'not *next* to one another, but on *top* of one another,' with meaning built up and up through the sequence. Complex ideas could thus be communicated very quickly, and metaphor and symbolism incorporated into film along with pure narrative. Both the content and order of the shots are important in achieving this communication. Some sort of order will be imposed on the shots in the viewer's own mind to derive meaning from them. There was debate among Soviet theorists as to whether this order is primarily logical or psychological, however, but its effect is undeniable.

in place. It took until 1898 for films to start putting shots together, and Robert W Paul's *Come Along, Do!* (1898) was one of the first to put two shots together. Paul's innovative reverse-crank camera incidentally allowed double exposure of films and 'trick' effects (Georges Méliès used one), but it was his cutting and splicing of different images together that would be more revolutionary.

Continuity editing

What Paul, and the first professional editor James Williamson, developed came to be called continuity editing. This stitches two shots that are linked by time or place to continue the story. A shot is any single piece of film. It could be as short as a single frame, or as long as the entire film (2002's *Russian Ark*, for example). The vast majority of shots have always been under ten minutes, the old length of a reel, but by the 2010s, average shot length was somewhere around 2.5 seconds. Shorter shots are popular in, and suited to, action movies, helping to communicate the fast pace of events. *Mad Max: Fury Road* (2015) offers an excellent example of short shots being edited expertly together to tell a coherent story – in this case, by keeping the action centred in the frame so that very quick cuts can be used without making viewers dizzy or disoriented.

An effective juxtaposition of shots can tell a story even without dialogue. This is the 'Kuleshov effect', where Russian filmmaker and theorist Lev Kuleshov found that viewers would project emotions onto a human face based on the shots placed next to it. So, they 'read' the image of a screaming face, followed by the action of a raised knife being brought sharply down, as a person being stabbed, even without ever seeing the knife touch flesh, as in Alfred Hitchcock's *Psycho* (1960). If we see a plane taking off in one shot, and then someone walking through an airport arrivals gate, we understand that they have travelled to a new city despite the ellipsis of time involved. Continuity editing creates a sense of temporal coherence that can be misleading (*Inside Llewyn Davis*; 2013) but can also carry a story along without huge swathes of exposition.

Types of edit

Types of shot combination include the 'match cut', where the edit takes place between two very similar shots. A famous example is that of a prehistoric bone spinning through the air matched with a futuristic space station in *2001: A Space Odyssey* (1968). A 'jump cut' is an abrupt transition, usually taking the viewer on a leap forward in the same timeline and scene to indicate the passage of time, especially when a series of these is used. 'Cross-cutting' or 'parallel editing' happens when the edit switches back and forth between two scenes, which tends to indicate that they are taking place at the same time, so between the three parallel battles at the end of *Star Wars: Return of the Jedi* (1983). A 'J-cut' or 'L-cut' is where audio from one scene carries over into the next after the image has changed, or appears before the scene to which it is attached. And images may be 'dissolved', 'faded' or 'wiped' from one scene to the next, instead of simply replacing one another. This is especially useful when the two are visually distinct, where the director or editor wants to add a bit of a flourish for any reason, or where there is a time passage between the two.

> **The most wonderful thing about editing is that you're given all this raw material and it's your job to make choices.**
>
> Thelma Schoonmaker, *The Visible Art of Editing with Thelma Schoonmaker*, 2021

Split screen

Most editing is sequential, but sometimes images are placed together side by side onscreen, or in a grid, to communicate actions taking place at the same time. The technique was used early in cinema history to great effect by Lois Weber in 1913's *Suspense*, where a mother and baby are shown at the same time as a home intruder creeping about their house. It was used wittily in comedies such as *Pillow Talk* (1959) and its homage *Down With Love* (2003) to show both sides of a phone conversation. Split screen also covers early cases where one actor appears twice in the same scene, as in *The Dark Mirror* (1946), where the camera could be locked down and the scene filmed twice, once for each character.

Non-linear and hyperlink editing

Continuity editing remains a hallmark of most mainstream filmmaking, but there are alternatives. Non-linear storytelling, perhaps obviously, sees the story unfold in non-linear ways, so that the timeframe is not intuitive. Think of Quentin Tarantino's *Pulp Fiction* (1994) or Christopher Nolan's *Dunkirk* (2017), which uses the normal rules of cross-cutting against the audience. This is a combination of writing, directing and editing that can allow for surprising revelations, leaving the viewer to do more work in untangling the story, but encouraging them to pay more attention to make sense of it all. An overlapping concept is hyperlink editing, a term first used by Alissa Quart in 2005 and popularized by Roger Ebert. This describes films with complicated or multiple narratives linked by theme or by a single event. Examples include Steven Soderbergh's *Traffic* (2000) or 2004's *Crash*. Both forms demonstrate how wildly creative editing can be, and how much it contributes to storytelling. Good editors, such as Anne V Coates, Sally Menke, Thelma Schoonmaker, Michael Kahn or Robert Wise, can make a good film extraordinary.

The condensed idea
Placing carefully chosen shots together

06 The close-up

A close-up shot is a huge advantage that cinema has over the theatre. At any moment, a director can emphasize a particular expression, or draw the viewer's attention to some specific detail of the scene. It allows for an almost surgical manipulation of attention, and is enormously important in both storytelling and in conveying a film's emotional impact. If theatre uses spotlights to direct a viewer's attention to a particular spot onstage, cinema has something more akin to a laser at its disposal.

The invention of the close-up is generally credited to British innovator Arthur Melbourne-Cooper in *Grandmother's Reading Glass* (1900), though fellow Englishman G A Smith also used the technique in *The Little Doctor* the same year, so it is not entirely clear who was first. However, it was popularized, and its use honed, by D W Griffith and his cinematographer Billy Bitzer, who used it to great effect throughout their silent shorts and into the epic storytelling of films like *Intolerance* (1916).

The two-shot

Close-ups are not the only important storytelling shot. A two-shot is, as it sounds, a shot showing two people. Think of the medium shot of Humphrey Bogart's Rick and Ingrid Bergman's Ilsa on the airfield in *Casablanca* (1942), for example. It is a good shot for establishing the relationship between two people, whether that is shaped by love or hate or something in between. Other examples include the two hitmen in *Pulp Fiction* (1994) and almost any shot of the protagonists in *When Harry Met Sally* (1989). If a close-up encourages us to think about a character's emotional state, the two-shot encourages us to think about the way these characters interact, thereby further illuminating both.

Coverage

Coverage has something of a bad name among directors. You will sometimes see interviews where a director sniffily claims never to shoot coverage. But it can be a useful tool. Coverage simply means that a scene may be shot from multiple angles – perhaps in a wide shot that covers everything, medium shots and some close-ups. This gives editors a lot of choice later, and helps with continuity issues, but can make films feel a little generic. Some auteur directors, including Quentin Tarantino, Christopher Nolan and Clint Eastwood, avoid shooting coverage, preferring to stick to a careful plan. Others, like Ridley Scott in recent years, will use multiple cameras and angles on a single scene, shooting fewer takes but with many angles on each one to play with in the edit.

How close?

How close is a close-up? Well, that depends. Take a human figure for reference. A medium close-up is sometimes called a 'two-button,' because you see the top two buttons of someone's shirt as well as their head and shoulders. A standard close-up might show only the head, or go as far as the top of the shoulders. A 'big' close-up shows the face, filling most of the frame, and an 'extreme' close-up might show only the eyes, or another facial feature. All of these serve different purposes. The medium and standard close-ups are more widely used, perhaps helping to establish a character's importance to a scene, but the big and extreme close-ups are jarring and tend to be used more sparingly.

The purpose of the close-up

The first, and most important, use of the close-up is to bring the audience into the emotion of the film. A smiling face filling the screen, or a tearful one, may provoke a matching response in the audience. It is a fact of human behaviour that we tend to mimic that of someone we are facing in order to form a connection with them. More obviously, a close-up shot of such an emotion emphasizes that that emotional state is important to the filmmaker and thus to us in the audience. If someone looks afraid, or joyful, we want to know why.

Close-ups may also be used for things hidden from other characters onscreen – someone slipping a gun into a pocket, say – or to emphasize that an item is important. There are repeated extreme close-ups of the One Ring in *The Lord of the Rings* films (2001–03) that make it seem of enormous significance (some of these even used an oversized prop to further enhance the ring's importance). A close-up could draw attention to some element of a character's costume, or of the set, or allow us to luxuriate in the perfect features of some love interest whose attractiveness must be established.

Uses of the close-up

Some directors are particularly known for their close-up shots. The extreme close-up was sometimes called a 'Sergio Leone,' after the director's penchant for extreme close-up shots of his characters' eyes in such films as *The Good, The Bad and the Ugly* (1966). Leone used

The 180-degree rule

This is an interesting cinematography guideline that helps establish the spatial relationship in a scene. Basically, it says that the camera should stay on one side of the imaginary line between two characters in a scene. Think of the diner scene in *Heat* (1995). It is as if the camera is stationed at one end of the table, turning back and forth between Al Pacino and Robert De Niro, so even when only one is in shot, we know they are looking at the other. If the camera suddenly shifted to the other end of the table, nearer the counter, our understanding of the spatial relationship between the two would be broken. This 'rule' is sometimes more of a guideline, especially when covering larger groups – but it is a useful start when planning complicated dialogue scenes.

close-ups to tell his stories with as little dialogue as possible, contrasting those intimate shots with long, sweeping wide shots. David Fincher uses extreme close-ups to draw audiences into the minute detail of his characters' worlds and to show a lock opening or a man shaving off his own fingerprints.

Alright, Mr DeMille, I'm ready for my close-up.

Gloria Swanson as Norma Desmond, *Sunset Boulevard*, 1950

Edgar Wright tends to use close-ups in montage for comic and storytelling effect. A precise series of timed cuts communicates Shaun's plans to survive a zombie apocalypse in *Shaun of the Dead* (2004), and a series of close-ups including a slamming car door describe Nicholas Angel's relocation in *Hot Fuzz* (2007). James Cameron uses close-ups in *Aliens* (1986) for a tooling-up scene, for example, while Steven Spielberg's trademark 'Spielberg face' is a tight shot that shows a character's wonderment at something happening off-screen, selling the awesome sight even before he shows the spaceship, dinosaur or other special effect.

The condensed idea
A feeling of intense intimacy with the people onscreen

07 Cinematography

Cinematography is the art that creates a film's look. The cinematographer, also known as the director of photography, DP or DoP, and their team will have responsibility not only for cameras, but also for lighting, and will work closely with the director and other department heads to coordinate the overall look and tone of the film. They will choose, or help to choose, the shots used for each scene, and will shape the film's visual storytelling.

In the wild days of early cinema, there was no specific DoP role: a filmmaker like Georges Méliès would probably create his own shots. However, within about a decade, cinematographers as we now know them had begun to appear, such as D W Griffith's collaborator Billy Bitzer, who together with the director developed backlighting and soft focus. As cameras improved, so did the options available for any given shot. Robert W Paul developed a rotating camera head to follow Queen Victoria's Jubilee procession in 1897, and this 'panning' camera and its successors allowed DoPs to follow a scene's action. The

Sven Nykvist

A regular collaborator of Ingmar Bergman, Swedish cinematographer Sven Nykvist is considered one of the greatest and most influential cinematographers of all time. He was a proponent of naturalistic lighting, typically using only one light source to avoid the sort of double shadow that might hint at posed photography. Outdoors, he found ways to capture light that communicated transcendence and spiritual awakening. He won two Oscars for his work with Bergman – for *Cries and Whispers* (1972) and *Fanny and Alexander* (1982) – but also shot for Louis Malle, Nora Ephron and Richard Attenborough in his 120-plus film career.

development of zoom lenses, dolly tracks and booms that allowed the camera to move, more sensitive film stock and more adaptable lighting all opened up new possibilities for cinematographers, as have digital intermediates and more sensitive digital cameras today. In the studio era, DoPs were sometimes constrained by a studio's house style and, more importantly, by their rushed production schedule, but Gregg Toland's use of deep focus in *Citizen Kane* (1941) is one example showing that innovation was still possible within that system. Nimbler cameras and more location shooting by the 1950s and 1960s allowed for the lush effects of Freddie Young's work for David Lean on films like *Lawrence of Arabia* (1962), before a switch to the more subdued hues of the 1970s New Hollywood work. There has, in fact, been a shift to darker images across film since the end of the studio era. Some of this is due to more sensitive film, allowing for lower lighting and a more downbeat tone than the sunniness of early colour films. But it is also a matter of style, and a chance to use minimal lighting to maximum effect.

> If I had the same style on every movie, it wouldn't be interesting. My style is to tell the story the right way each time.
> Vilmos Zsigmond, *FilmCraft: Cinematography*, 2012

Cinematography and technology

The options available to a DoP have steadily widened as cameras and technology have improved. There is a major technical component to cinematography: the DoP must ensure that the film is in focus, sufficiently well lit to make out the characters and any pertinent details, not over- or under-exposed so that the image is accurate, framed so that all the requisite action is visible, and planned so that the viewer's eye is drawn to the most important elements in any shot. However, the DoP also has a huge amount of influence on a film's look and style. They may create or emphasize certain colours, or lean heavily on a given style of shot to communicate the mood of a piece. Think of Christopher Doyle's vibrant reds in the films of Wong Kar-wai, or the darker framing of Gordon Willis (*The Godfather*, 1972) and Vilmos Zsigmond (*The Deer Hunter*, 1978).

A good cinematographer will work hand-in-glove with the director on the film's look and feel. Some directors spend decades working

I Am Cuba (1964)

This otherwise relatively obscure Soviet Cuban documentary coproduction is often cited by cinematographers for its astonishing cinematography by Russian DoP Sergei Urusevsky. One particularly bravura sequence sees the camera travel along a street, up a building, through a window into a cigar factory and back out through another window, apparently floating over the street. Prior to the invention of Steadicam, this was accomplished by attaching the camera to the operator's vest and hooking him to a series of pulleys and cranes, but it has been cited by filmmakers including Martin Scorsese as one of the greatest cinematographic feats of all time.

with the same cinematographer for this reason – for example, the Coen Brothers and Roger Deakins. Other directors sometimes act as their own cinematographer, and include Steven Soderbergh, Robert Rodriguez and Nicolas Roeg. The cinematographer will often also collaborate closely with costumes and production design to achieve a unified overall effect, particularly if the film is a more stylized one and requires a uniform colour palette or strong lighting design. Their contribution may also be key in choosing locations; some of the trickiest work any cinematographer will face lies in making a small, dark or awkward-to-access location look good on camera.

Style and collaboration

A cinematographer's work is bespoke to each film, designed around that film's setting, era and tone, so that even the same cinematographer and director will create wildly varied results. Compare Steven Spielberg and DoP Janusz Kaminski's *Schindler's List* (1993), *Saving Private Ryan* (1998) and *West Side Story* (2021), for example. The format and look of a film might even shift during its course, to signal different eras or different character moods (Spike Lee's *Malcolm X* in 1992 and Danny Boyle's *Steve Jobs* in 2005), even changing film format or colour. That said, some cinematographers are particularly known for handheld work, long tracking shots or strong use of colour, so there may be at least preferences alongside their endless adaptability.

Cinematography has historically been an overwhelmingly male profession, with apologists claiming that DoPs tend to come up through the camera department and spend the early years of their career doing heavy lifting of equipment. At the time of writing only about 6 per cent of DoPs are female. However, this is beginning to change with efforts to diversify the profession and newer, lighter digital cameras removing some of the old excuses. Female cinematographers leading the way include Ellen Kuras, Rachel Morrison, Ari Wegner and Polly Morgan. Cheaper and less expensive cameras, such as phone cameras, have generally made it possible to achieve impressive cinematographic effects with extremely small budgets and good taste (Sean Baker's *Tangerine* in 2015 and Steven Soderbergh's *Unsane* in 2018).

The condensed idea
Lighting, shot selection and expert camera control

08 Mise-en-scène

This French phrase is much bandied about in film criticism, but is rarely defined. Literally, it means 'put on stage', and indeed its roots are in theatre. There, it refers to the staging of a play: the decision to set *Hamlet* in the present day, say, or to sing *Madame Butterfly* over a pool of water. Similarly, in film terms, it refers to everything that is within the frame of the image, and how it is organized. A film's mise-en-scène encompasses how it looks and even how it moves, and the phrase's sheer breadth means it is a useful catch-all, despite its slight air of snootiness having seen it fall from favour in everyday critical discussion.

In its broadest definition, mise-en-scène is everything a director has decided to do with a script. What has been given prominence in the frame, what fades into the background, and what was that background in the first place? Has the director chosen to stage a love

The Red Shoes

British filmmakers Michael Powell and Emeric Pressburger adapted the fairytale of *The Red Shoes* in 1948 into a story of artistic creativity, obsession and desire. All their films are beautifully put together, but this, with its striking Technicolor cinematography by legendary director of photography Jack Cardiff and heightened production design by Hein Heckroth, is particularly memorable. The 17-minute ballet set piece at the heart of the drama begins rooted in the proscenium of a stage but swiftly expands outwards to impossible dimensions via soundstages and SFX trickery, getting swept up in the dance just as our heroine, Victoria Page (Moira Shearer), is swept away herself. As she loses herself, so the audience goes with her, before a tragic outcome takes us all back to reality with a crash.

scene against a battle, for example, or a shootout in a hospital? An infinite number of choices will have been made in adapting a script page (or whatever the source material may be) to the screen, so a discussion of the mise-en-scène essentially involves unpacking all of those choices and trying to derive meaning from them.

While the term is sometimes used in reference to a single frame or image, it more usually encompasses a series of images and cuts that form one scene or sequence, so that it allows analysis of everything that a director has done to tell their story in a synecdoche of the film as a whole.

> As for mise-en-scène, when it corresponds precisely with the spoken word, when there is interaction, a meeting point between them, then the image is born.
>
> Andrei Tarkovsky, *Sculpting in Time*, 1985

Framing, lighting and setting the scene

Mise-en-scène refers to the framing of a shot (is it a close-up? A wide shot? A two-shot?) and how (if) the camera moves during the scene. It also encompasses production design and the way that the setting is used to convey meaning to the viewer: Are we in a shack or a palace? A moving vehicle or a spaceship? Connected with that setting may be the lighting and how that is used to move our focus around a frame. We might see one character spotlit, for example, while another lurks in the shadows (or, Michael Myers in *Halloween* style, emerging horrifyingly from them). There are also questions of costume to consider, not only in the showier sort of costume drama or fantasy film, but also in more realistic tales. The black suits and ties of *Reservoir Dogs* told a story of cool, and harked back to an earlier age; the outfits of *Barbie* not only placed us in her sugary world, but provided a nostalgic hit for half the audience. Hair and make-up matter too, from the extreme looks of an *Eraserhead* or a *Hairspray*, or the creature make-up of *The Shape of Water*, to the more naturalistic but striking glow given to the stars of romcoms. The mise-en-scène can therefore also encompass performance, although that's usually discussed separately.

Technically it's also part of the creation of mood and tone, whether an actor is screaming wildly or barely moving a muscle. Time and depth plays a role, too: the famous long shot of Sherif Ali (Omar

Wes Anderson

If you want to see a poster boy for extravagant mise-en-scène, look no further than Wes Anderson. His early films had some trace of realism, but even in *Rushmore* (1988) and *The Royal Tenenbaums* (2001), he used those perfectly centred shots of his heroes staring solemnly into camera, and by *The Grand Budapest Hotel* (2014), he had almost entirely abandoned realism for a storybook world of saturated colours and deliberately artificial locations, creating a noticeable contrast to both the rundown modern-day scenes at the same hotel, and the horrors of the looming war. In *The French Dispatch* (2021), a love-letter to journalism, he changed his filmmaking style for each constituent story, while his meditation on grief and loss, *Asteroid City* (2023), takes place in an almost two-dimensional desert that, at times, seems to come from a Looney Tunes cartoon. There's always a method to his mise-en-scène, and even when there's a huge contrast between fantastical setting and more sombre tone, it brings his films to life.

Sharif) in *Lawrence of Arabia* (1962) establishes both the vast emptiness of the desert and some hint of the time taken to travel across it. Finally, editing may be included in the mise-en-scène. Stanley Kubrick used shorter shots, on average, for the comedy *Dr Strangelove* (1964) and more stately, longer shots for the cerebral *2001: A Space Odyssey* (1968), to cater to different genres, while famous 'single shot' films like Alfred Hitchcock's *Rope* (1948) inevitably move at a different pace.

A similar concept to mise-en-scène had been discussed in the film journal *Sequence* in the late 1940s, where critics and theorists expounded ideas around 'film poetry': the idea that the style of a film was as crucial to its success as its content. So, a simple story could be elevated by expert and considered storytelling, using the image to give power to the story's meaning and emotion. Just to add a little confusion to proceedings, the term 'mise-en-scène' is occasionally used in screenwriting, there to define the blocks of scene direction that a writer may include in a script to set a scene or move from one moment to the next.

The director as architect

The wider use of the term – and this will come as no surprise to any cineaste reading – has origins in the French magazine *Cahiers du Cinéma*, and the critics there, a list that included future filmmakers François Truffaut and Jean-Luc Godard. It was a key concept in their overarching argument that a director – rather than, for example, a screenwriter – is the principal architect of a film. The endless questions of style, pacing, colour, gesture and movement were almost all issues determined by a director, so an emphasis on mise-en-scène was inevitably one that highlighted the director's role and importance; in this reality, it's almost entirely synonymous with 'directing'.

This focus was initially controversial. Penelope Houston, the then-editor of British film magazine *Sight & Sound*, considered it almost offensive to suggest that cinema was about 'spatial relationships' rather than the human situation. But the two are not mutually exclusive. The mise-en-scène contributes to the emotion of a scene, and the film as a whole.

The condensed idea
Every decision the director makes

09 Sound and soundtrack

Even in the silent era, films were usually accompanied by a soundtrack. A musician, playing anything from a pipe organ to a violin, would accompany the images onscreen and attempt to enhance the effect with music that was lively, suspenseful or sad as the need might be. The arrival of sound therefore merely codified some aspects of the film experience but, crucially, it also allowed the addition of dialogue and narration.

The birth of sound

Studios hankered for true sound films. There were early sound experiments by Thomas Edison and Alice Guy at Gaumont, but it was tricky in those days to fully synchronize the sound to the image. In 1919, Lee de Forest developed the first composite print, with the sound information stored optically on the same strip as the images, allowing both to play at once. This was initially tricky and difficult to manage, but technological improvements during the 1920s made it more practical and affordable. This optical track was eventually replaced by magnetic sound in the 1950s and then by digital sound in the 1990s.

The start of the sound era is generally dated to Warner Bros' *The Jazz Singer* in October 1927. Star Al Jolson was a singer and vaudevillian who performed six numbers in the film, as well as dialogue scenes, though his performances in blackface have aged less well than the film's synchronized sound. It was a sensation, so studios scrambled to re-equip for sound, and encouraged exhibitors to do the same. A vast investment was required, but these films were initially sold at a premium to audiences, offsetting some of the cost, and a slew of dance movies and lively musicals capitalized on the new format. Quickfire comedies also came into their own, allowing witty, fast-talking talent such as Mae West and the Marx Brothers to replace much of the old silent movie slapstick. Similarly, more complicated stories could be told now that dialogue did not have to be squeezed onto intertitles: Anita Loos, who had been famous for her verbose intertitles, was far better suited to writing dialogue in the likes of *Red-Headed Woman* (1932). Major stars going into sound became a selling

Leitmotif

Leitmotif is a term adopted from classical music, where it is associated with works such as Wagner's Ring Cycle, to refer to a musical phrase that is used to denote a particular character, thing or place. One of its first uses in film was for Peter Lorre's serial killer in 1931's *M*. Since then, the idea has been popularized in film by composers such as John Williams, who uses at least 55 leitmotifs across his *Star Wars* scores, and Howard Shore, who has something like 130 across *The Lord of the Rings* trilogy.

point: 'Garbo talks!' was one advertising slogan for 1930's *Anna Christie*, which was indeed Garbo's first talkie.

There was some resistance to sound. Early sound recording was delicate and difficult, and it could not easily be combined with the sort of camera movements that had been available in silent cinema (the development of the boom mic, usually credited to director Dorothy Arzner, helped with this). Some silent directors, such as Fritz Lang, felt that sound left less room for artistry and captured reality too precisely. Charlie Chaplin held out until 1940 and *The Great Dictator*, preferring his old style until he had too much to say. It also meant that films could not travel the world as easily, and initially saw film fragment along language lines, until dubbing was introduced in 1932.

By 1930 the Academy Awards had added a Best Sound category, and has at times recognized Best Sound Mixing, Best Sound Effects Editing and Best Sound Editing as different categories, as well as having awards for Best Score (also sometimes subdivided by genre) and Best Song. As the number of categories suggests, sound quickly became essential to movies: even 'silent' films in modern times, such as 2011's *The Artist*, use a soundtrack.

Soundtracks and score

Music recorded specifically for film existed even before sound films. The first film score dates back to 1908, when the composer Camille Saint-Saëns wrote a score for *The Assassination of the Duke of Guise*, but it became more popular after the almost entirely new score by Joseph Carl Breil for *The Birth of a Nation* in 1915. This was distributed to cinemas alongside the film, and viewers in bigger cities could hear a custom score alongside the film. But with the sound era, the best musicians in the world could record music heard with the film everywhere. This was one of the guiding ideas behind Disney's *Fantasia* (1940), but a sweeping orchestral score soon became standard for epic films such as *Gone with the Wind* (1939), soundtracked by Max Steiner.

> Sound is rarely used dramatically these days and yet the world is becoming auditive. . .The visual is the only sense that gives us detachment, objectivity, rationality. All the other senses are irrational, discontinuous and disconnected, especially sound.
>
> Fritz Lang, interviewed for *Sight & Sound*, 1967

Foley art

One of the most important elements of a soundtrack is not the dialogue or music, but the sound effects – footfalls as a character walks, the crack of a ball being hit or the smacking lips of a kiss. Sometimes this is recorded on set, but in many cases, because of background or camera noise, or due to special or visual effects, it must be created later by 'foley' artists. These talented people must create sounds that match the image onscreen, sometimes using considerable imagination: stabbing a watermelon, perhaps, instead of a skull.

Most films in the modern era have a specially composed score or a soundtrack made up of existing music – pop songs, for example. Some use both. Either way, the music is designed to enhance the emotion of a scene and perhaps enhance storytelling or tension. John Williams' score for *Jaws* (1975) hugely adds to the film's tension and effect, but, in contrast to some of the rest of Spielberg's storytelling, never wrong-foots us. The *Jaws* theme only appears when the shark is there. An eerie musical cue can also be used to put us on edge, however, and indicate that other dangers might be nearby.

Composers may start work on a film at script stage, but more often they work relatively quickly and quite late in the day, using a rough cut to figure out themes and overall sound and then refining the score as the director locks the final edit. Scoring and sound mixing (putting together and balancing the score, sound effects and dialogue) are usually one of the final steps in completing a film, giving it much of its final emotion and impact.

The condensed idea
Synchronized music, dialogue and sound effects

10 Special effects

Special effects (SFX) encompass anything done physically or in front of the camera to create an extraordinary effect onscreen. This might (and often does) include setting things on fire, creating fake snow or rain, or building creature effects for animal or monster characters. It may also involve constructing huge rigs to create spectacular car crashes or sink ships, or miniature cities for monsters to destroy. The most impressive effects tend to be a combination of techniques, sometimes alongside optical or visual effects as well, to create a truly seamless unreality.

SFX pre-history

The first SFX were mostly visual effects like the 'stop trick' and the use of mattes, but naturally stage experts in special effects and magicians also began to work on film, creating puffs of smoke and flashes of light. Film pioneers such as Robert W Paul developed cameras that could be reverse-cranked, allowing for multiple exposures and, for example, the addition of a ghost to *Scrooge: Or, Marley's Ghost* (1901). Willis H O'Brien started animating with stop-motion models in the 1910s, and in France, some of Georges Méliès' films involved elaborate combinations of stop tricks and stage magic. Mack Sennett, for his Keystone Kops films from 1912, would replace mannequin doubles with actors to show people surviving impossible falls, and play with cranking speed to make very safe near-car crashes look thrillingly dangerous.

> At one time, our job consisted of telling the director what he couldn't do. Today, everything is possible. Our roles consist of helping them tell their story in the best way possible using the techniques that are available to us.
>
> John Dykstra, *Special Effects: An Oral History* by Pascal Pinteau, 2004

As filmmakers' ambitions grew, special effects came to play a key role. Tracks and pulleys allowed a magic carpet to fly in 1924's *The Thief of Baghdad*, and jiggling gelatin served as the parting of the Red Sea in Cecil B DeMille's *The Ten Commandments* (1923). Fritz Lang created a city in miniature for 1927's *Metropolis*, with flying cars travelling among its towers on wires, and integrated actors with carefully positioned mirrors. The Universal monster movies involved sometimes spectacular creature prosthetics, and Lon Chaney built a reputation as the 'man of a thousand faces' precisely because of his expertise in make-up effects.

The monster hit *King Kong* (1933) was only possible because of O'Brien's continued refinement of his miniature models, using rabbit fur and a posable metal frame to create the titular ape. The 1930s also saw the development of rear projection, to allow driving shots for example, and the 'travelling matte', which allowed the replacement of even moving images from one frame to another. The sci-fi films of the 1950s and 1960s saw further leaps forward, with a pneumatically controlled giant octopus in *20,000 Leagues Under the Sea* (1954), sophisticated water effects in 1956's *The Ten Commandments*, and the inspired use of rotating cameras and extraordinary ape prosthetics in

Stan Winston

Winner of four Academy Awards and a frequent collaborator of James Cameron, Steven Spielberg and Tim Burton, Stan Winston is one of the most important figures in SFX history. After a make-up apprenticeship in the late 1960s at Disney and a decade spent working in TV and on films like *The Wiz* (1978), Winston really rose to prominence in the 1980s with his extraordinary creature designs for *The Thing* (1982). He found a key collaborator in James Cameron, working on *The Terminator* and creating the massive Alien Queen for Cameron's *Aliens* (1986). He also created *Predator*'s (1987) titular baddie, worked on *Edward Scissorhands* (1990) and *Batman Returns*' (1992) The Penguin, and built the dinosaurs for Spielberg's *Jurassic Park* and the robots for his *A.I.: Artificial Intelligence* (2001). Late career work included Jon Favreau's *Iron Man* in 2008, the year he died. He's remembered as an SFX pioneer and someone who shaped sci-fi filmmaking, in particular.

Stanley Kubrick's *2001: A Space Odyssey* (1968). Meanwhile Ray Harryhausen, O'Brien's successor, took miniature work to new heights in films such as *Jason and the Argonauts* (1963) and *Clash of the Titans* (1981).

One great leap

The disaster movies of the 1970s further pushed special effects, with films such as *The Poseidon Adventure* (1972), *The Towering Inferno* and *Earthquake* (both 1974) demanding large-scale dazzle and careful control of fire, water and motion. But the technology developed for *Star Wars* in 1977 had to meet far greater challenges. The motion-controlled camera systems used to film its dogfights and spaceships were a landmark in SFX working with VFX to create a realistic whole, with the SFX crew creating ships, droids, speeders and monsters and the VFX team helping to remove the visible rigs required to make them operate.

Stunts

A stunt is really a special effect. It is, after all, a physical process used to safely do something that is actually very dangerous on camera. Some flying scenes or 'wire-fu' martial arts involve large and complicated stunt rigs, while fire effects may involve setting fire to (carefully protected) stunt performers. The first stunt performers appeared in the early 1900s, often daring young men doing something foolhardy for free. The first record of a paid stunt performer ($5) comes from 1908's *The Count of Monte Cristo*. Nowadays expert fight choreographers and stunt coordinators can travel the world and sell their skills for considerably more. Audiences have a near insatiable appetite to see people do impossible things onscreen, but thankfully safety rules and protective measures have significantly improved since the silent era, when many stunt performers died or suffered life-changing injuries. Aside from fight scenes and falls, stunt people may control speeding vehicles, perform fire or water scenes, or double for actors playing sports and especially extreme sports.

Special effects set-ups grew more and more impressive through the late 1970s and 1980s, with flying rigs in *Superman: The Movie* (1978) helping you believe a man could fly, and models like Stan Winston's *The Terminator* (1984) exoskeleton helping sell the idea that a man might be killed by a robot.

The VFX challenge

A tipping point, where computer VFX began to seriously challenge physical SFX, came on Steven Spielberg's 1993 *Jurassic Park*. SFX luminaries, including Stan Winston and Phil Tippett, had been working on the dinosaurs for months when Spielberg realized that some of the bigger shots could best be accomplished by Dennis Muren's VFX team. The VFX team got much of the credit for the dazzling film that resulted, though the convincing reality of their shots is aided considerably by the close-up animatronic models.

In the latter half of the 1990s and early 2000s, led by George Lucas's *Star Wars* prequels, there was a sense that VFX had permanently displaced SFX, beyond make-up and prosthetics, for all world-building and creature work. However, its death was declared prematurely. Films like the *Harry Potter* series (2001–11), with SFX by John Richardson, showed that sometimes the most convincing results are due to a careful blend of SFX and VFX, and even *Star Wars* came back to its SFX roots for the sequel trilogy that started in 2015. Big budget films in the 2020s are more likely to trumpet their real-world elements than their VFX work (sometimes unfairly to VFX teams), but a sense that reality is best achieved by the creation of physical effects now dominates once again.

The condensed idea
Physical trickery that happens 'in camera'

11 Visual effects

Visual effects, or VFX, encompass any element that is done in addition to the image captured by the camera on a live-action set. While special effects might, say, create a monster suit that someone wears to chase other actors around the set, visual effects could add the image of a monster to the live-action footage afterwards. Handling everything from spaceships to superheroes, doing 'invisible' set extensions and clean-ups, and even digitally de-aging actors, modern visual effects play a huge role in the filmmaking ecosystem.

Early days

Initially, of course, VFX were far more limited. What is generally accepted as the first visual effect was achieved in 1895 in a seconds-long film called *The Execution of Mary Stuart*. There, actor Robert L Thomas, as Mary, took position on the headman's block, the director stopped the camera and had everyone freeze, and replaced Thomas with a dummy. The camera started again and the dummy was beheaded for a (relatively) seamless effect. This technique came to be known as a 'substitution splice' or 'stop trick' and was popularized, to more expert effect, by Georges Méliès just a few years later.

Méliès had a background in stage magic, and proved a key pioneer in both visual and special effects. His career, between 1896 and 1913, included science fiction and fantasy films and saw him develop innovative techniques such as multiple exposures and dissolves. During those frantic early decades of cinema, filmmakers used the stop trick, split-screen photography, time lapse and anything else they could think of to dazzle and thrill audiences. The combination of live-action filming and delicate stop-motion animation created such classics as 1933's *King Kong*, animated by Willis H O'Brien, already a veteran who'd been working on stop motion since 1915. His techniques were further honed by his pupil, Ray Harryhausen, in work that involved stop-motion animated miniatures cut together with live-action footage. Harryhausen would refine his techniques into the 1980s. At heart, however, most VFX still involved splicing two images together, but the complexity of the images possible grew steadily, and technology like motion-controlled cameras opened new horizons. Stanley Kubrick's *2001: A Space Odyssey* (1968) pioneered sophisticated front projection and cameras on special tracks to shoot repeated images that could be composited together. George Lucas' *Star Wars* (1977) and Jim Henson's *Muppets* films (1979–84) and *Labyrinth* (1986) required extremely sophisticated compositing techniques to remove animators from the frame and place the results of work against a realistic background.

Going digital

The next true revolution in visual effects came in the 1980s with the birth of digital animation. A growing number of computer scientists, led by the likes of Ed Catmull, pioneered 'texture mapping' and other ways to make images digitally on computer and animate them. George Lucas established a computer graphics department at Lucasfilm to develop this new technology, led by Catmull and a former Disney animator called John Lasseter. They created the first digital character, a stained-glass knight brought to life for one scene in *Young Sherlock Holmes* (1985), before founding Pixar Animation Studios. Throughout the 1990s a generation of VFX artists pushed these techniques forward until not only environments and monsters, but entirely digital lead characters could appear onscreen.

Alien beings such as Jar Jar Binks (*Star Wars: Episode I – The Phantom Menace*; 1999) and Gollum (*The Lord of The Rings* trilogy; 2001–03) could mingle relatively seamlessly with their human co-stars. This was achieved via 'performance capture', where actors were put in body suits covered in reflective points (or ping-pong balls), with little reflective dots covering their faces. With the help of a small inward-pointing camera attached to the head to capture every facial expression, these actors could then create a performance on set alongside their human co-stars, under a director's control, before handing off to the VFX team to transfer that performance to a creature in the finished image. These techniques were further honed and refined by James Cameron's team for his *Avatar* films (2009, 2022), which saw human-level emotion transferred to a huge cast of blue cat-like aliens.

By the early 2000s, some films were wholly or partially made on 'digital backlots' – bare green screens against which worlds could be created around human stars. These sometimes created odd, uncanny effects, however, and a strange sense of weightlessness. By the late 2010s and early 2020s, via Alfonso Cuarón's *Gravity* (2013) and TV's *The Mandalorian*, the green screen had been relegated to a secondary role and replaced with 'The Volume', a gigantic, wrap-around screen

Uncanny valley

The human eye is much quicker to accept obviously cartoonish or alien imagery than near-human fakes. Scientists speculate that the instinct may have come from the need to spot outside invaders, or people infected with rabies, but we instinctively reject anything almost-human looking. This has proved problematic in the eternal quest for more realistic human characters in VFX: something almost right is much more likely to pull us out of the narrative than something openly artificial. VFX artists have created 'digital doubles' of human stars for moments of stunt spectacle or superheroics, sometimes with incredible success, but are yet to have a digitally created, fully human character perform for any significant length of time.

Matte painting

There is one kind of visual effect that, traditionally, was captured by the camera on set: matte painting. This might involve a glass pane with a realistic image painted on it, placed in front of the camera at an appropriate distance to create the right illusion and framing a section of the image where actors move. Famous examples include the warehouse full of crates in *Raiders of the Lost Ark* (1981), or the Emerald City in *The Wizard of Oz* (1939). This technique essentially still exists, but there's no longer a physical painting most of the time. Nowadays sets are expanded with a digital matte rather than a physical painting.

on which digital images created by VFX artists could be projected to provide both a reference for actors (and lighting VFX) but, increasingly, an alternative to old-style static scenery. While The Volume is enormously helpful for the right project, it too has been hit with accusations from film critics of unreality. The biggest modern films therefore tend to try to mix VFX and SFX, to find the right mix of in-camera realism and movie dazzle. The advent of AI assistance in VFX compositing, and the use of games engines such as Unreal, has somewhat reduced the enormous time and cost of VFX in filmmaking, but it remains one of the largest ticket items in a film's budget.

The condensed idea
If you can't shoot it, draw it

12 Film formats and aspect ratios

Serious audio-visual obsessives take endless joy in comparing and contrasting different film stocks, cameras and, in particular, frame ratios – that is, the shape of the image we see onscreen. Some are practically square; others wide and panoramic. Most are relatively standardized, because film is an art form that relies on certain technologies to run, but parts of the image can be boxed off if a filmmaker really wants to cut down on the space available. Or, since the widescreen revolution of 1953 and the development of IMAX in the 1970s, filmmakers can make the image significantly bigger and more detailed than ever.

Format development

The appetite from audiences for fresh film content was high almost from the beginning, so it was in the interests of filmmakers and

Smell-o-Vision and 4DX

There have been attempts at stranger and more theoretically immersive film formats over the years. 1960's Smell-o-Vision released smells in the cinema at specific points in the film, starting with *Scent of Mystery*, and was successful enough to inspire rivals like Smell-o-Rama and AromaRama. John Waters parodied the trend with his 'Odorama' scratch-and-sniff cards for *Polyester* in 1981. The idea was largely dismissed as a stunt – few films had a sufficiently major smell element to justify the cost – but it has been popular in some theme park film experiences that incorporate smell, moving chairs, water and wind effects in their filmed content. It also plays a role in 4DX, which debuted in 2009 and which similarly introduces movement, wind, rain, strobes and smell into special seats in standard multiplexes worldwide.

distributors to make sure that their product could be played as widely as possible. That meant figuring out a standard. It was one of the biggest players of early cinema history who essentially forced everyone else into line. Thomas Edison owned most of the US patents on cameras and film stock, and from 1902, he enforced those patents via endless lawsuits, to the point where most of his competitors gave up and negotiated a deal to use his cameras and stock. The result was the Motion Picture Patents Company in 1908, and an agreement that film would be 35mm wide, with four perforations to each frame. Together the member companies controlled two-thirds of the US market and strangled film production, banning the sale of films to distributors in favour of rentals, and limiting film length to a single reel. However, Edison's patents expired in the early 1910s, and the company was judged a monopoly in 1915, forcing its dispersal. By then, however, most silent film had settled into a 4:3 aspect ratio – that is, slightly wider than it is tall. That, however, would not be the only option forever.

Ratio rivalry

The next attempt to fully standardize film came with sound-on-film stock in 1929, when the Society of Motion Picture Engineers settled on a 1.33:1 aspect ratio, roughly the same as 4:3, with room for the optical soundtrack on the film strip. That aspect ratio was also set for 8mm film, which was standard for home shooting for much of the century, and which was the first format used by most would-be directors. In 1932, however, the Academy of Motion Picture Arts and Sciences considered alternatives and settled on 1.375:1, the 'Academy ratio'. This became the default for all studio films until 1952 and was widely imitated around the world.

But in 1952, Cinerama debuted with a spectacular 2.59 ratio on a wide, curved screen that aimed to fill the audience's entire field of vision. These images involved using three synchronized cameras and then projectors, which created problems. Cinerama films could not use a zoom lens, because it distorted the image too much, and worse, had a small sweet spot in the cinema where the picture worked best. So, while it created a sensation, studios largely rejected Cinerama and developed their own widescreen formats instead, using an anamorphic lens that could shoot a wide field without distracting distortions. By that time, filmmakers felt the pressure to offer something big and spectacular that could not be replicated at home on TV. In the 1950s, 20th Century Fox trumpeted its CinemaScope format, which was 2.55:1, for its Biblical epic *The Robe* (1953); Paramount introduced 1.66:1 for *Shane* (1953); MGM and Disney opted for 1.75:1; Universal and Columbia tried 1.85:1. All of these were achieved by chopping the top and bottom of the frame rather than by using specialist cameras. The vast majority of widescreen cinema now is 1.85:1, while HDTV tends to be cut to 1.78:1 (also called 16x9).

The bigger screen

From the 1950s on, then, widescreen became the standard language of cinema and almost entirely replaced the Academy ratio, which is now chiefly used for artistic effect. It has been chosen to simulate old TV, as in Gus Van Sant's *Elephant* (2003) and Pablo Larrain's *No* (2012), and a filmed stage production (Joel Coen's 2021 *The Tragedy of Macbeth*); Andrea Arnold, who used it on *Fish Tank* (2009), called it 'the perfect frame for a person'. Widescreen is the general rule otherwise, except in IMAX. This large-screen format, developed from

Format switching

Film formats can be used in creative and narrative ways. Christopher Nolan's *The Dark Knight* (2008) used IMAX for its action scenes but zoomed in to a more traditional 35mm aspect ratio for dialogue scenes – not least because the IMAX cameras at that time were too noisy for use in enclosed spaces and for dialogue. Andrew Dominik frequently shifted aspect ratio and film stock, during *Blonde* (2022) to match the still photos and historical footage on which he based the film's look, while Danny Boyle similarly used different film for different time periods in *Steve Jobs* (2005) going from newsreel-like 16mm to 35mm to digital. Beyond a personal aesthetic preference, formats can thereby change a viewer's experience of a film.

1967 to the early 1970s, uses a 1.34:1 ratio but a vastly bigger film stock – not only 70mm wide but 15 perforations high, in contrast to the 4:3 format's four perforations, for example. Initially used chiefly for documentaries, IMAX began working on smaller, lighter and (crucially) quieter cameras in the 2000s, enabling native IMAX use in feature film as well.

There have also been attempts to make film a three-dimensional experience for as long as film has existed. It was not until 1952 that there was significant success in 3D film, with the dual-strip 3D of *Bwana Devil* using Polaroid filters to show each eye a slightly different image for a 3D effect. 3D remained a novelty in the 1960s and through a 1980s revival, but was popular enough to see improvements in the technology involved, such as IMAX's real-colour 3D glasses. By the digital era of the 2000s, it was possibly to process an image for 3D after it was shot traditionally, a cost-effective way of making movies, and films such as James Cameron's *Avatar* (2009) showed the potential for immersion with well-designed, native 3D. However, a flood of imperfectly converted 3D films, and attempts to force audiences to choose 3D led to a decline, so it is once again a niche choice.

The condensed idea
Determining the shape and size of a frame

13 Frame rates

The phenomenon of the persistence of vision means that our eyes retain an image for a small fraction of a second after the image is removed. That is the mechanism that explains all cinema: show us a sequence of similar images quickly enough and they can appear to flow seamlessly from one to the next. But how many images are needed to create this illusion, and how fast do they need to move? It took a little while to figure that out.

At 10 to 12 frames per second (fps), we perceive individual images; somewhere above that, we start to experience movement between images. However, all frame rates are not created equal. In the silent era, many cameras were hand-cranked, and frame rate could be anywhere from 16 to 24 frames per second. Early on, 16fps became an industry standard: cameras and projectors were calibrated so that a steady cranking rate of two turns per second gave 16fps of usable film. The rate sometimes changed from one scene to another to fit the 'mood' of the piece: Charlie Chaplin, for example, sometimes slowed the film in the camera for action scenes to create a more manic, madcap effect when projected at a normal pace.

Working with sound

By the mid-1920s, the artists who already took film seriously were pushing for a higher standard frame rate, because it significantly reduced 'flicker' on the screen as the projector moved from one image to the next, and gave a smoother effect. The American Society of Motion Picture Engineers recommended a standard rate of projection at 21fps. This brought them into conflict with producers and distributors, who saw all that extra film as extra cost. After all, going from 16fps to even 21fps required an extra 15 ft of film per minute.

When sound arrived in the late 1920s, however, the frame rate had to be standardized. A sound recording was placed on the same film strip as the image, so the image had to be stabilized to match the sound because inconsistent frame rates would lead to variations in the sound's pitch or failed synchronization. It was not long before 24fps became the industry standard because it offered a stable sense of movement and almost eliminated onscreen flicker, but also allowed

Animation 'on twos'

Often, in hand-drawn animation, each painstakingly created image would be duplicated for use in two frames, so that animators only had to draw 12fps to achieve a realistic effect. This was known as a character being shot 'on twos' and was entirely standard. If the action was particularly fast-paced, they might be animated 'on ones', with a full 24 drawings per second. On the other hand, cheaply made Saturday morning cartoons might only have moved 'on threes' or 'on fours', giving them an extra edge of artificiality. Such variations can be used artistically. In *Spider-Man: Into The Spider-Verse* (2018), hero Miles Morales initially moves 'on twos' as he swings but progresses to moving 'on ones' as he gets to grips with his powers. The character of 'Spider-Punk' Hobie in the sequel *Spider-Man: Across the Spider-Verse* (2023) uses the method to create a sense of asynchronicity: he is animated 'on threes' and sometimes even his own jacket is animated at a different rate, giving him a subtly out of sync quality in keeping with his refusal to conform to the rules of The Man.

the space to record sound efficiently alongside the image. The rate also reflected standard electric motor speeds at the time, based on the frequency of mains electricity.

While 24fps has remained standard for film as well as most smartphones and streaming into the present day, television uses slightly higher rates. Europe and most of Asia use 25fps on the PAL format and the Americas and Japan use 30fps on NTSC. This is, again, partly due to standard mains electricity. Films shot on 24fps but shown on TV therefore used to be very slightly faster, with a slight difference in pitch of the sound, but modern corrective technology means that this is no longer noticeable.

The arrival of digital cameras

In recent years the dominance of 24fps has been challenged. The advent of digital cameras and projection means that the physical limitations of film no longer make higher frame rates prohibitively difficult to manage or fund. Higher frame rates can reduce flicker and blur even more, and create a smoother, brighter experience. A higher frame rate can also help with three-dimensional images, which could create eye strain because they require brighter light to compensate for the fact that the images are flickering from one eye to the other.

Some technologically minded filmmakers have therefore started to push the limits. Peter Jackson made *The Hobbit* films (2012–14) at 48fps but found it largely rejected by audiences. Higher frame rates can appear cheap or soap-opera-like to audiences trained at 24fps; the screen seems to glow more than usual and the lack of flicker and motion blur can even be alienating. Ang Lee released *Billy Lynn's Long Halftime Walk* in 2016 and *Gemini Man* in 2019, the first of which was

Douglas Trumbull

Special effects guru and director Douglas Trumbull, who did extraordinary work on *2001: A Space Odyssey* (1968) and *Close Encounters of the Third Kind* (1977), advocated for higher frame rates for decades. In the late 1970s and early 1980s he researched audiences' emotional reactions to films shot at different frame rates, even hooking people up to an EEG while watching various clips, and claimed that emotional impact was highest at 60fps. His Showscan format debuted in the 1980s and used 60fps to impressive effect, but never took off because of the cost of retrofitting cinemas to use it. Instead, it was mostly adapted for use in immersive theme park rides. He tried again in 2014, introducing a 3D, 4K, 120fps system called Magi, that used an innovative system to provide 60 images per second, per eye, but it has not taken off.

partly shot at 120fps and the latter entirely so. Neither were particularly warmly received. However, there was a more positive response to James Cameron's *Avatar: The Way of Water* (2022), which was rendered at 48fps for certain scenes and embraced by audiences – possibly thanks to the brightly lit surroundings of its alien setting.

Higher frame rates may yet become the norm, to go with our increasing use of 4K definition (and higher). Games are already moving towards higher frame rates to reduce blur during fight scenes, which may change the expectations and tastes of viewers, and the technological barriers to higher frame rate use are only falling. For now, however, the feeling remains that 24fps isn't broke, so there's no need to fix it.

> We're using [high frame rate] to improve the 3D where we want a heightened sense of presence . . .For shots of just people standing around talking, [high frame rate] works against us because it creates a kind of a hyperrealism in scenes that are more mundane.
>
> James Cameron on *Avatar: The Way of Water*, *Variety*

The condensed idea
Seeing movement that isn't there

14 The movie star

The first movie stars were created by fans, not studios. In the early silent era of the 1910s, actors were not even credited by name, and studios were taken aback when fan mail nevertheless started to arrive for some of their regular players. There were attempts to resist this cult of personality and maintain control of the situation, but gradually journalists discovered actors' names or studios released them – or the actors announced their identities to the world – and the tide turned in favour of these nascent stars. Audiences began to follow their favourites from film to film, and actors began to leverage their appeal for bigger salaries, more control of their careers and a larger slice of the pie. From then on, studios realized they would have to use film stardom rather than suppress it.

The movie star as a phenomenon swiftly eclipsed previous categories of celebrity. Unlike authors, actors could be vividly and visually present in front of audiences. Unlike stage and musical stars prior to the advent of television, they could be all over the world at any given time. Film stars were more glamorous, generally, than sports stars but had the same thrilling career ups and downs. They were also gifted one particularly potent tool: the close-up created a sense of intimacy with their audience that other formats could not match. Even before the advent of sound, audiences could sense what an actor was thinking as their face filled the screen. Less than 20 years after the birth of cinema an entire fan-fuelled publishing industry had grown up around film, following the lives of stars and examining their work in detail.

The studio star

As the studio era began and industrialized film production took hold, stars became an asset to be exploited. Promising young actors would be put under contract to a studio where they would be groomed, trained and moulded for stardom. They might be educated in diction and deportment, or dressed and coiffed according to studio preferences. Their very names might be changed – Archibald Leach chose to become Cary Grant; Lucille LeSueur became Joan Crawford following a fan magazine poll – their hairlines lifted or their faces reshaped to fit the screen. Roles were often chosen to lean into a particular persona: James Cagney playing gangsters and G-men; Ingrid Bergman in saintly roles; Doris Day as a career girl. Studio press officers would concoct stories about them for the voracious appetites of the fan magazines, and studio fixers would ensure that any less desirable stories about them were buried for as long as their box-office power held firm. They were even tradeable commodities: stars under contract to one studio could be loaned to work for another at a significant mark-up on their salary (they would not receive a share of this).

This was not always an oppressive system. Very big paydays awaited some stars; at one point Mae West was the highest-paid woman and second highest-paid person in the United States, for example (behind only William Randolph Hearst). But it could be stifling. Women who got pregnant outside marriage (or even inside

The first stars

In 1908, Florence Lawrence and Florence Turner received fan mail addressed simply to 'Biograph Girl' and 'Vitagraph Girl', respectively. Lawrence and her husband tried to leverage this enthusiasm for higher pay and perks such as a personal make-up table. The couple was fired in 1910 as the studio tried to keep control, only to be snapped up by future Universal Pictures founder Carl Laemmle. Lawrence and her husband later set up their own studio, Victor, to capitalize on her fame. Vitagraph Studios, meanwhile, bowed to the inevitable and made Turner the face of the company for more than five years. In 1913 she sailed to England and took her star power to international level, establishing Turner Films in the United Kingdom while also touring vaudeville and variety shows. While neither woman maintained their star power into the late silent era or sound days, each had shown that film stardom was a significant force.

Box-office draws and box-office poison

'Star power' or 'bankability' measures how attractive a star's name is to audiences, a measure of how much a Mary Pickford or a Tom Cruise adds to a film's box-office take. The potency of Hollywood stars was once measured by the Independent Theatre Owners Association, which, in May 1938, took an advertisement out in trade paper *The Hollywood Reporter* to brand some stars 'box-office poison' and argue that they were overpaid relative to their appeal. The list included established stars Joan Crawford and Katharine Hepburn, both of whom continued to have successful careers long afterwards. Hollywood stars are not the only box-office royalty worldwide, however: the likes of Jackie Chan, Shah Rukh Khan and Takeshi Kitano have also had decades-long careers and phenomenal success around the world.

it, in the case of Ava Gardner) might be pressured to have an abortion or dropped from their contract. Studio doctors were known to dose stars to keep them working: most notoriously the young Judy Garland, because the studio-mandated regime of uppers and downers that kept her working long hours as a teenager contributed significantly to her early death. Contracted stars were pushed into films and roles they felt unsuitable or actively harmful to their careers, and only a few (Bette Davis, for example) raised enough hell to push back on those decisions. Stars such as Olivia de Havilland, in a landmark court case, and Marilyn Monroe began, with some success, to challenge the studio system in the 1950s and 1960s, arguing for greater autonomy and control over their careers. Gradually the contracted star gave way to freelance status, with actors navigating their own career paths, aided (or not) by agents, managers and lawyers.

Modern times

In recent years, the status of movie star has come under unprecedented pressure. Citizen journalism and the ubiquity of phone cameras and social media has removed many of the filters between star and audience, making it more difficult to achieve and maintain megastar status. Studios now seek to rely on 'IP' or intellectual property-based franchises rather than star vehicles, which has also reduced the bargaining power of big names: Sherlock Holmes or The Hulk can be recast in a way that Gene Hackman or Julia Roberts cannot. However, even today, the star remains potent. The right star name – potentially Zendaya, or The Rock, for most of the 2010s – can still come close to guaranteeing a certain level of financial success, and the undefinable quality of star charisma can make the difference between a good film and a great one.

**The condensed idea
On the big screen, charisma matters**

15 Animation

Animation is often discussed as if it is a genre, a brightly coloured format for children and suspiciously enthusiastic adults. However, it is best considered as a medium, because it can be used to tell stories in any genre. There are extraordinarily good animated horrors, dramas and erotic thrillers; there are animated films from all over the world, going almost as far back as cinema itself.

Arguably all cinema is animation. The usual definition is that animation occurs when a series of still images is created frame by frame to create the illusion of movement. Tiny, incrementally different

Walt Disney

Walt Disney's passion for animation, which could be experimental at times (1940's *Fantasia*, for example) was combined with a conviction that it could be a mass-market art form. Disney worked for decades to figure out what (particularly American) audiences wanted to see. His studio's early years endured a boom-and-bust cycle, with almost as many flops as hits, but Disney crafted a blend of classic fairytale material, entertaining animal or fantasy characters to appeal to young kids, and an appealingly clean and simple style that, with variations, still dominates children's animation today. The Disney style inspired generations of artists, including notable filmmakers like Tim Burton and John Lasseter, and Disney's astute business head – building his studio around catalogue titles, alongside endeavours in TV, merchandising and theme parks – set a pattern that was decades ahead of its time.

images can thus create extraordinary life; the only difference from 'live action' is that these images do not show unaltered actors, things or places, but rather characters, situations and visuals created by drawing (using handheld implements or computers), puppets, paper cutouts, clay or silicone models, or live-filmed images that have been augmented or changed by additional processes. The last, called 'rotoscope' animation, was developed by Max Fleischer. A living actor or action is filmed and then the resulting image is drawn or painted over with matching animation. It is a technique that has been used for decades: some fragments of Disney animation were rotoscoped, as were films like Ralph Bakshi's *The Lord of the Rings* (1978) or Richard Linklater's *A Scanner Darkly* (2006). A more sophisticated version of the same process continues in the 'performance capture' of James Cameron's *Avatar* (2009), or Gollum, in Peter Jackson's *The Lord of the Rings* trilogy (2001–03). There, human performances are transferred in painstaking detail to non-human creatures, interacting with humans in live-action fantasy worlds. The difference is ultimately one of degree rather than definition.

The alternative to the relative realism of rotoscoped forms was the 'squash-and-stretch' style used by Fleischer but taken to greater heights in the 1930s by Disney. This takes greater advantage of the hand-drawn format to exaggerate movement and make characters more appealingly comical, with a bouncing motion that deforms a character's body before stretching it back into shape; it remains one of the basic principles of a lot of children's animation in particular.

A slow start

Animation took a decade or so to become popular after public exhibition began. The appeal of early films was their lifelike quality; animation smacked of early moving images like zoetropes and perhaps seemed like a backwards step. But it did exist. Englishman Arthur Melbourne-Cooper made a series of animated films in 1899 with matchstick figures playing volleyball or appealing for money to fight the Boer War. By 1907 the partly animated likes of The Haunted Hotel had appeared, using stop-motion models to create outlandish effects. In 1908, France's Émile Cohl produced the two-minute long *Fantasmagorie*, arguably the world's first fully hand-drawn animation, since it's entirely based on line drawings. Nine years later, Italian-born

Argentinian director Quirino Cristiani made the first animated feature, *El Apóstol*, a political satire (now lost) that used cardboard cutout characters. The oldest surviving feature animation, *The Adventures of Prince Achmed* (Lotte Reiniger), dates back to 1926, but it was the enormously popular *Snow White and the Seven Dwarfs* (1937) from Walt Disney that changed the calculus for animation permanently. Disney's survival as a company, and occasional monster successes, proved animation's viability as a commercial enterprise, and if European and Japanese studios pushed the art form forward, Disney and his American successors proved its economic engine.

To CG or not to CG?

The arrival of feature-length, computer-animated films with Pixar's *Toy Story* in 1995 was a leap forward just as the art form threatened to become calcified. Computer graphics genius Edwin Catmull had partnered with traditionally trained animator John Lasseter in the mid-1980s to begin work on CG animation (their early efforts are visible in *Star Trek II: The Wrath of Khan* (1982) and *Young Sherlock Holmes* (1985)). The commercial and critical success of *Toy Story* began a new era for animation, because computers made it possible to animate more complex surfaces (think of the detail of the marble throne room in 1991's otherwise hand-drawn *Beauty And The Beast*) and adventures possible. The state of the art of VFX drove the stories these films could tackle: initially, hard and shiny surfaces were easier to handle so we got stories about toys and bugs. Then the computer effects improved to handle water and fire, so we got stories about fish, and fairytale monsters. By the 2010s, almost anything was possible with enough money and time.

Despite initial reports of its demise, hand-drawn and stop-motion animation has survived and even thrived alongside the big CG films, thanks to companies like Studio Ghibli (*Spirited Away*; 2001), Cartoon Saloon (*The Secret of Kells*; 2009), Aardman (*Wallace & Gromit* films; 1989–2024) and Laika (*Coraline*; 2009). Many of these have adopted some elements of CG enhancement or, in the case of the stop-motion houses, 3D-printed elements, while CG artists often use live-action references. The future of animation may therefore end up something of a hybrid, with a mix of puppetry, CG, stop-motion and live-action elements in work by new companies like Swaybox Studios.

Anime

The most culturally powerful animation in the world, and one of the most dominant pop cultures full stop, comes from Japan's anime tradition. The term 'anime' is generally used to describe Japanese-made animation, and a few other productions in the Japanese style, though within Japan the term describes all animated art worldwide. Animation in Japan dates back to 1917, but the now-characteristic style, with its big eyes and bright colours, dates back to the work of manga artist Osamu Tezuka and his imitators in the 1960s. Anime masterpieces such as Katsuhiro Otomo's *Akira* (1988) and a string of hits from Hayao Miyazaki and Studio Ghibli established the art form in cinemas worldwide, but it's the long-running TV shows like *Neon Genesis Evangelion* and *Dragon Ball Z* that have cemented its place in the culture beyond cinema screens.

The condensed idea
Bringing inanimate creatures to life onscreen

16 Documentary

The very first films were documentaries, simple shots of everyday life: a train arriving in a station, workers leaving a factory. Such non-fiction remained popular even after the advent of fiction filmmaking, with documentarians travelling the world to bring back footage of far-off places and different ways of life. For a time, the genre seemed largely subsumed by newsreels, or sidelined as an oddity by the glitzier business of features, but it came back to prominence as a filmmaking practice from the 1950s onwards. It's probably fair now to consider documentary as a medium rather than a genre, a way of filmmaking in its own right. There are documentaries that are funny, scary and even, arguably, science fiction (Asif Kapadia's *2073*; 2024), so the form is more elastic than it might seem.

Documentary film per se never entirely went away. In 1922 an early feature documentary, *Nanook of the North* from director Robert J Flaherty, showed that fascinating documentary subjects could become box-office hits – though, at a time before the strict separation of fiction and non-fiction, it relied on some staged scenes to bring its portrait of Inuit life to a wider audience. The most widely cited documentary filmmaker of the 1930s is Leni Riefenstahl, whose propaganda films *Triumph of the Will* (1935) and *Olympia* (1938) for Adolf Hitler were hailed for their technical precision and ambitious scope even as they glorified the dictator's monstrous regime.

Cinéma vérité vs direct cinema

The cinéma vérité movement of the 1950s and direct cinema movement of the late 1950s and early 1960s brought a zeal for realism into the documentary arena. Cinéma vérité allows for a greater acknowledgement that the filmmaker exists, perhaps even as a character in the film, and can involve provocation of the documentary subject by the filmmaker. The direct cinema style is stricter and has become the more dominant force: there, the aim is for the filmmaker to disappear almost entirely, using minimal lighting and camera equipment, and capturing sound in the moment or not at all. The filmmaker aims to distract the subject as little as possible from their normal behaviour. Both forms reject re-stagings and fictionalized elements. However, there is by no means a hard-and-fast line between the two: both descriptions have been applied to the works of Jean Rouch (*Chronicle of a Summer*; 1961), Robert Drew (*Primary*; 1960), DA Pennebaker (*The War Room*; 1993) and the Maysles brothers (*Grey Gardens*; 1975) who seem to identify more with the 'direct' definition, to name but a few.

Alternative approaches

A slightly different, archive-based style was developed by Ken Burns, who made acclaimed documentary series for television as well as Oscar-nominated films such as *Brooklyn Bridge* (1981) and *Statue of Liberty* (1985), where still images and footage were cut together, stitched with a voiceover by an actor or actress. Alex Gibney belongs to a similar school, using interview voiceover and narration in his documentaries *Enron: The Smartest Guys in the Room* (2005) and *The Armstrong Lie* (2013). Gibney is also notable for his rejection of a journalistic 'view from nowhere' objectivity, arguing that good documentary does not reject a solid point of view. The more impressionistic style of Chris Marker's *Sans Soleil* (1983) also appeared, to address more subjective and even subconscious views. Arguably 2024's animated Lego documentary *Piece-by-Piece* from director Morgan Neville is also a barmier example of the impressionistic tradition.

Reconstructions, meanwhile, had not left the form for good: Errol Morris used them extensively in *The Thin Blue Line* (1988) to present an alternative account for a murder case whose conviction he had come to doubt (that documentary led directly to the overturning of the conviction of it subject, Randall Dale Adams). They're also used extensively in the Oscar-winning *Man on Wire* (2008), with an actor playing a younger version of the documentary's subject, Philippe Petit, and partial narrator.

Modern documentaries

While documentary has been influenced by mainstream filmmaking as cameras have improved and ambition and budgets have grown, it has been influential in its turn. The handheld, shaky-cam effect of some direct cinema efforts has been mimicked in war movies such as *Saving Private Ryan* (1998) and action movies such as *The Bourne*

Michael Moore

One of the most successful documentary makers of the 1990s and 2000s is Michael Moore, who uses factual filmmaking and some contrived situations to deliver political and social satire. Moore puts himself front-and-centre of his films; he is not simply a narrator and commentator like, say, Werner Herzog, but a contributor to the narrative. His efforts to secure an interview with General Motors CEO and president, Roger B Smith, to talk job losses and capitalism form the backbone of his first documentary, *Roger & Me* (1989). Moore made a bigger impact with *Bowling for Columbine* (2002) and *Fahrenheit 9/11* (2004), dealing with US gun violence and the War on Terror respectively. The former won him an Oscar for Best Documentary; the latter became the highest-grossing documentary of all time.

Supremacy (2004) to enhance the immediacy and realism of their set pieces, giving the viewer a sense of immersion in something that is really happening. The 'talking head' format used to stitch together the narrative of many documentaries – where an interview with a subject is used to explain or advance the narrative of a documentary – has been recreated in fiction, particularly in mockumentaries, but also in feature films based on non-fiction material, such as *The Big Short* (2015).

Documentary is sometimes treated as the poor cousin of feature filmmaking, afflicted with shoestring budgets and often a place where female directors are encouraged to work in lieu of competing for feature jobs; Alma Har'el and Alice Diop both got their start there. But the gap between feature and documentary can be bridged, and documentary careers can run alongside feature filmmaking: look at Agnès Varda or Martin Scorsese. The scope and breadth of documentary filmmaking remains vast. Some tell intimate stories of a single person (*Amy*, 2015; *Free Solo*, 2018) or explore an obscure mystery (*Searching for Sugar Man*, 2012). Some have world-changing

Mockumentaries

The basic format of documentaries is recognizable enough, yet flexible enough, that it has been extensively adopted to tell fictional stories. Notable 'mockumentaries' or 'mock docs' include *This is Spinal Tap* (1984) or even animated penguin comedy *Surf's Up* (2007). There, actors playing characters may deliver talking-head commentary direct to camera about events onscreen, which are often captured on apparently handheld cameras, or actors may interact with one another or members of the public in a real or faux-reality setting. Typically, much of the dialogue is improvised or semi-improvised. In the case of Sacha Baron Cohen's *Borat* (2006) and *Brüno* (2009) films, for instance, the other party does not always know they are talking to an actor.

ambitions (*An Inconvenient Truth*, 2006) while others seem to come directly from their maker's peculiar interests (*My Octopus Teacher*, 2020). While television has co-opted some documentary energy and developed its own peculiar forms, such as reality TV, documentary film remains a powerful and popular medium on the big screen.

The condensed idea
Stories from the real world

17 Distribution

Distribution is perhaps the least understood part of the film industry by viewers, because when it works they do not have to think about it and when it does not work they are generally not aware what they are missing. Distribution is the link between filmmakers and audiences, the means by which films get to cinemas or, increasingly, to other outlets – collectively known as exhibitors – and thence to the eyes of paying customers. A distribution company may be part of the studio that makes the film, so Warner Bros or Disney, for example, distribute their own films as a rule. But a distributor might also be a separate entity, buying independently made films at festivals or following private screenings, or acquiring the rights to foreign films to sell in a given territory, or re-issuing old films that might not otherwise be seen.

The VHS boom

The VHS or 'video home system' was introduced in 1976 and became ubiquitous throughout the 1980s and 1990s, after defeating its more expensive rival Betamax in the market. A cheap way to distribute films with reasonable quality sound and video, the VHS format fuelled a boom in low-budget filmmaking and provided the viewing material for generations of film fanatics, not least through video-rental stores. Entire film industries, such as that of Nigeria, were built on VHS, as were genres like horror's 'video nasties', low-budget efforts based on shock and gore. Digital Video (or Versatile) Disc, or DVD sales, finally overtook VHS sales in 2003, and in 2006 the last film released on VHS (*A History of Violence*; 2005) marked the end of an era (Blu-ray's attempts to replace DVD, in contrast, were derailed by streaming). By then, however, VHS had changed the calculus for film production by introducing the era of on-demand film viewing at home.

Early days

Initially, film distribution was a somewhat haphazard affair of travelling shows with scratchy film reels, but very quickly an industry sprang up that allowed filmmakers to stay in one spot and keep working, while others hustled their work onto screens. In the United States, films were sold state-by-state, with one payment to the filmmaker by the exhibitor, who would then play the film as many times as they wanted and hold the profit. Obviously, that was not satisfying for studios, who might underestimate the appeal of their film and sell it at too low a price. The alternative that developed was a 'roadshow' model, where exhibitors paid a percentage of the ticket price to the distributor and thus shared the proceeds. This is roughly the system that works today, with profits from ticket sales shared between the exhibitor and distributor.

In the studio era, the major studios either owned, or were owned by, cinema chains, so they could confidently block book their own cinemas and exhibitors could be relatively sure of a steady flow of new films to keep audiences engaged. Studios could also pressure cinemas, by withholding big, attractive films unless theatres also agreed to book less-appealing efforts. This was a form of 'vertical integration', with Hollywood studios controlling every step between the production of the film and its appearance in front of audiences. However, the Paramount Decree of 1948 broke up this comfortable monopoly (for the studios), forcing studios to sell off, or break off, their US cinema chains and compete with one another, and with independent and foreign films, for screens. This eventually led to a significant increase in the variety of films available, both in the United States and around the world, and somewhat democratized filmmaking.

You've got to be worth paying for all the time.
Netflix co-CEO Ted Sarandos on streaming

Towards today's system

A more open distribution model resulted. Independent film producers often aimed to sell the distribution rights to their films even before going into production, attaching a star name or two and selling rights country by country at events such as the Cannes Film Festival's Marché du Film to raise a portion of the budget. This reduced risk for financiers and guaranteed material for distributors well in advance of release. Specialist distributors grew up who might focus on horror, or arthouse films, or of course pornography. The rise of home entertainment on VHS, DVD and Blu-ray fuelled these specialist labels and established that there were niche markets to be exploited by those who could distribute their films quickly, cheaply and widely.

In recent times, studios have been accused of pressuring cinema chains to devote a certain number of screens to big films in return for access to blockbuster content, or pressuring exhibitors to book smaller films in return for permission to screen commercially valuable bigger efforts. The Paramount Decree was subject to 'sunsetting' in 2020, freeing the studios to once again invest in cinemas and bringing criticism from independent US cinema owners that they were left open to monopolistic practices. Streaming services, and studios with their own streaming services, arguably have vertical integration already today, controlling every step from greenlighting films to their release. This means that they keep a much larger percentage of profits in-house but may limit a film's reach.

Streaming

The first media stream was the Théâtrophone of the 1880s, which allowed subscribers to listen to opera down the phone line. In the 21st century, advances in networking, data compression and home and personal computing power have made it possible to 'stream' films directly to viewers, wherever they are, via streaming services and apps. In the late 2010s, the 'streaming wars' between such giants as Netflix and Amazon, and traditional film studios such as Disney and Paramount, saw them compete for subscribers who would essentially be captive audiences for their product. An explosive growth of streaming services followed, with a particular spike in use during the Covid-19 pandemic, and the streamers concerned invested heavily in original and exclusive content to entice viewers. Growth stalled post-pandemic, but by then the streamers were thoroughly entrenched in most of the world.

International variation

Distribution practices differ around the world, and some countries intervene with quotas and subsidies to support local film production. The United Kingdom was the first territory to introduce a quota for local films, in 1927, initially set at 7.5 per cent of films but later raised to 20 per cent of films exhibited in the United Kingdom. This led to the production of cheap local films nicknamed 'quota quickies', which did not enhance the reputation of British film either at home or abroad. French cinema introduced an import quota that demanded one local film be made for every seven imported, and has seen more success in propping up its local industry as a result. Similar rules into the present day have kept local production high in countries from Brazil to South Korea. China, too, limits the number of foreign films it permits, granting fewer than 40 licences for such films each year. Generally, however, distributors are guided by the market, always searching to connect films to the audiences who will pay for them.

The condensed idea
Getting films from filmmakers to viewers

18 The silent era

The silent era was a time of vast and rapid change in film. The transformation in cinema's first 30 years rivals the microchip revolution for its sheer dizzying speed. It took film from its emergence as first a novelty and then a mass-market art form in the first two decades of the 1900s, through its climb to cultural relevance and economic force, to the arrival of sound in the late 1920s, traditionally dated to the release of *The Jazz Singer* in 1927.

When cinema began in 1895, films were no more than a couple of minutes long. By the mid-1920s Erich von Stroheim's first cut of his epic *Greed* (1924) would come in at about nine hours (it was cut to just under two and a half for release). Filmmakers moved from static cameras and single shots to pans, close-ups and zooms, used to striking effect in 1927's *Wings* and *It*, with Clara Bow. The roles of director, screenwriter, editor and producer, all amorphously interchangeable at the beginning of the era, coalesced into separate, specialized tasks. Interestingly, there were typically two credits for what we now consider screenwriters: one for the scenarist, who wrote the stories, and another for the author of the 'intertitles', or title cards, with dialogue or explanatory text (lip readers might pick up more dialogue, which was recited on set but not transcribed). Many films in the silent era were coloured, usually by hand, while it was common practice to have live music accompaniment, and even sound effects in bigger venues. In Japan, it was not unusual to have live *benshi* narration for silent films, which kept the silent era going there well into the 1930s.

> I never approved of talkies. Silent movies were well on their way to developing an entirely new art form. It was not just pantomine, but something wonderfully expressive.
>
> Lilian Gish

In the 'novelty' era, barriers to entry were relatively low. Cameras and film stock were the biggest costs, but audiences were forgiving and willing to pay for even short, simple movies. As the silent era progressed, dedicated studios with artificial lighting became the norm, while longer running times and more complicated edits sent film costs spiralling. Particularly popular actors became stars and demanded their worth. Early experiments importing Broadway stars to film demonstrated that the qualities necessary for film stardom were distinct from those of theatre, and it was initially very much trial and error to find out who had the requisite magic – for example, Rudolph Valentino and Mary Pickford. Cinema culture spread, with fan magazines chronicling the lives of the stars and directors giving interviews to discuss their work.

Hollywood triumphant

By the early 1920s, almost all independent film studios in the United States were crowded out of business by what was now Hollywood (where the industry had virtually decamped during World War I). Los Angeles proved more hospitable to the new industry than the East Coast had been. Filmmakers and studio heads were further from interference by the purse-string holders in New York, there were no established unions to argue with, and the clear desert light was a huge boon to outdoor production. Meanwhile, around the world, other national film industries emerged in countries that included Egypt,

How to define a silent film

It might seem obvious, but not all silent films are silent. Some Charlie Chaplin films made after 1927, such as *City Lights* (1931) and *Modern Times* (1936), are dialogue free but do have a soundtrack. The choice not to add speech was an artistic one rather than one born of technical limitations. So, a "silent" movie may refer to a film from the era before 1927, whether or not it has an original or newly written score, and also to films without dialogue, such as 2011's silent-era pastiche *The Artist*, Jacques Tati's 1953 comedy *Mr Hulot's Holiday* and even animations such as 2019's *A Shaun The Sheep Movie: Farmageddon*.

Russia, France, Germany, the United Kingdom and China, though all were outgunned by the United States, or were damaged by their own overproduction (in the case of Denmark, for example).

The impact of World War I had a huge effect on the nascent art form. Audiences around the world soared, as people sought the latest developments in the newsreels that were shown on cinema screens (such as the 1916 British documentary *The Battle of the Somme*) or tried to escape the war in Charlie Chaplin comedies or Pickford melodramas. But it was when the war ended and the Roaring '20s began that cinema soared.

Cinema as art

The perception that cinema was a low-class entertainment for the masses and not for anyone of serious character or education softened as its storytelling power grew. Films such as the hugely racist *The Birth of a Nation* (1915) and revolutionary *Battleship Potemkin* (1925) were generally hailed as masterpieces. Filmmakers such as Carl Theodore

Dreyer (*The Passion of Joan of Arc*; 1928) and Abel Gance (*Napoléon*; 1927) showed the medium's scope and ambition, while directors such as Lois Weber preached the moral authority of cinema as an art form and its capacity for progressive social change. Meanwhile, crowd-pleasing filmmakers Chaplin, Pickford, Buster Keaton, Mack Sennett, Mabel Normand and more took comedy to new heights, bringing the most polished of vaudeville skills to the screen and sometimes adding in trick photography to extend a joke beyond its real-life physical limits.

It is hard to give a full account of the silent era of cinema because the vast majority of silent films have been lost or damaged. The cellulose nitrate used for film at the time was highly flammable and delicate, and films faced high levels of attrition. Worse, a conscious attempt was made to downplay the era when promoting the early 'talkies'. In order to convince theatre owners to spend the money on sound upgrades, studios engaged in a campaign to mock silent film, even recutting silent movies with comedy soundtracks to ridicule the films and their makers. However, what has survived shows vast variety and innovation, and huge strides forward in visual storytelling that continue to shape what we see today.

The condensed idea
A time of extraordinary innovation

19 The studio era

The studio system is a catch-all term for a way of working that came to dominate Hollywood from the mid-1920s until the 1960s, though its high point passed long before that. Its signature feature was the contract: filmmakers and stars were hired by studios not for specific films, but for a specific length of time. The studio would then assign work to them during that time, ideally keeping stars and crew members shooting as much of the time as possible, with directors and writers churning out material to keep them busy. The point was to industrialize film production and maximize output for an apparently insatiable public.

The studio system therefore worked something like a film factory. Personnel were brought in on contracts following a successful screen test or breakthrough role at another studio or, occasionally, on stage. Writers were hired from anywhere they could be found, with many coming from newspapers, where speed was a priority. In 1925 Herman Mankiewicz, the future screenwriter of *Citizen Kane* (1941) wrote a telegram to playwright and reporter Ben Hecht saying, 'Millions are to be grabbed out here and your only competition is idiots. Don't let this get around.' Directors sometimes worked their way up from acting or editing jobs, and sometimes merely hustled themselves into work. That was largely the attitude to young go-getters as Hollywood grew almost overnight into a huge industry.

> I don't want good. I want it by Tuesday.
>
> Jack L Warner (attributed)

Putting the 'industry' in 'film industry'

The studios quickly standardized an 'A-picture' and 'B-picture' divide between prestige works (which commanded higher ticket prices in big city theatres on a first release) and the cheaper, quicker-to-make films that kept local cinemas full all year round. Smaller studios of the time such as Columbia would often specialize in B-pictures, hoping for a big return on a relatively small investment. Many studios between the 1920s and 1940s owned, or were owned by, a cinema chain, allowing them to block book their own wares into their own screens and create a vertical monopoly between production and viewers. Independent filmmakers did exist, but they could rarely be sure of finding cinemas to screen their work, since studio-owned chains effectively controlled the market. This also stopped foreign films from finding much foothold in the United States.

Studios made whatever they thought would sell, but some did have specialities, or areas of particular strength. Warner Bros, for example, built itself up around crime pictures, with gangsters and G-men leading a distinctly masculine line-up. MGM marketed itself on prestige, buying buzzed-about books and theatrical hits for adaptation and boasting that it had 'more stars than there are in heaven'. Paramount also relied on star names, whereas Universal found success with its 'monster' movies in the early 1930s. Disney, of course, was always about animation.

At first, the studio system did not particularly prioritize or value directors. They were there largely to oversee a shoot, and often moved on to their next project before the film's edit was finished. However, there were always exceptions to this rule, especially in the prestigious A-pictures where the director's artistry was a selling point for the film.

United Artists

It is worth noting that some star names resisted the studio system. In 1919, Charlie Chaplin, Mary Pickford, Douglas Fairbanks and D W Griffith set up their own 'studio', United Artists, with the aim of controlling and profiting from their work. The quartet had some trouble raising the finances necessary for their films, managing only five films a year for their first five years instead of the 20-odd they had aimed for, but by diversifying into distribution by buying theatres and bringing aboard independent producers such as Samuel Goldwyn, the company managed to prosper. It has undergone multiple changes of ownership and management, but the name survives as a production entity to the present day.

Such names as Ernst Lubitsch, John Ford or Frank Capra could press for their own priorities even within this system, with considerable authority to push for their own choice of cast, crew, script and shooting location. However, the studios were already wary of what would come to be called auteurs, stung by the cost overruns of artists like Erich von Stroheim or F W Murnau in the silent era, so that even the most powerful directors were kept in check. One means to do this was to keep production based, as far as possible, in a company's own soundstages and on studio backlots, under close supervision by executives and accountants. Tales of cost overruns on the Italian shoot of 1925's *Ben Hur*, for example, scared a generation of film executives into keeping directors under a watchful eye.

The erosion of the system

The cosy relationship between cinema chains and studios and the practice of block booking were finally brought to an end with the Paramount Decree in 1948, which stopped studios from owning cinemas and opened up cinemas to independent distributors and filmmakers (it was phased out by the US Department of Justice in 2019). That significantly eroded the power of the studios to fill cinemas with whatever they wanted. From that time on they would have to compete with independent and foreign films for screens, and could not be sure that all their films would have a cinema release. It marked the beginning of the end of the studio era. By the late 1950s, half of US films would be made by independent producers, even if the studios then distributed their work. The era of contracts and industrial-style production was over, although the studios themselves survived as powerful production entities and major players in the film market. However, open to competition from independent and foreign film, and from TV, they would soon find themselves struggling to hold on to the mass audiences they once considered standard.

The condensed idea
Systematizing and streamlining filmmaking

20 The Production Code

In 1915, the United States Supreme Court ruled that films were 'commercial products' rather than art. As a result, for the next 40 years they were not eligible for free speech protection and could, at any time, be made subject to government censorship. It was not until the 1950s that this decision was overturned and cinema was legally recognized as an art form. That interim saw film studios desperately seeking to avoid government interference in their output, resulting in a self-censorship regime called the Motion Picture Production Code, aka the Hays Code or, simply, the 'Code'. The good news is that it fended off the federal censorship the studios feared; the bad news is that it established certain perverse storytelling standards that continue to reverberate today.

The early panics around film were as often physical as moral. The flammability of early celluloid was a huge concern, as was the

The Code and race

Of all the negative consequences of the Production Code, perhaps the most devastating was its effect on Black actors and characters. With all hints of interracial romance strictly forbidden, the careers of Black stars such as Dorothy Dandridge and Lena Horne were fatally limited. They could not play a love scene unless it was with a Black man, and the studios had little appetite for a film with two Black leads. Often, they were shuffled off to a single throwaway musical scene that could be cut from the film before it was shown in Southern states.

tendency of small-time distributors to set themselves up in basements and other spaces without proper fire exits or safeguards. But the obvious power and popularity of cinema quickly created more existential terrors – namely, the prospect that this new fad might have a deleterious effect on society's morals. Churches and groups such as the Woman's Christian Temperance Union in many countries, but especially in the United States, expressed concerns that women and children would watch violent or sexual content and become delinquent or depraved as a result.

The case for censorship

By the early 1920s, local censorship boards seemed inadequate to the task and 36 US states started to seriously consider film censorship legislation. Hollywood studios forestalled this threat by bringing in morality clauses to govern the behaviour of their highest-profile names, and also by hiring William Hays, a former Postmaster General of the United States and Presbyterian elder who was put in charge of the new Motion Picture Producers and Distributors of America, later the Motion Picture Association of America (MPAA). It would be his task to clean up Hollywood.

Hays persuaded most of the states considering censorship to drop their plans, and instead started to dictate what Hollywood should and should not adapt. In 1929, he started work on the Motion Picture Production Code, written the following year but only enforced from 1934, after the incoming Roosevelt administration again threatened censorship. The Code barred 'excessive kissing' and all sex, or any implication of sex outside marriage. Skimpy costumes and swear words such as 'hell' were banned, as was childbirth (depictions of its reality might, it was feared, put women off). There was a requirement that religious figures be portrayed respectfully, and that criminals be punished by the end of the film. Homosexuality, relationships between people of different races and true crime were all forbidden. Interestingly, it also prevented the negative depiction of certain foreign countries and events, to avoid cinema causing any diplomatic incidents (for many years, this prevented an RMS *Titanic* movie being made). Finally and most devastatingly, a catch-all principle was that no film should 'lower the moral standards of those who see it,' which gave the Code's enforcers considerable leeway.

Challenges to the Code

The Code assuaged the concerns of the moral majority, for the most part, but artists pushed back on it almost from its inception. Mae West, who had just made a splash in Hollywood when the Code's enforcement began, would include a few obviously unacceptable lines in her scripts to give the censors something to focus on, and then use her trademark sly wit to turn apparently innocent quips into double entendres. Hitchcock got around the ban on lengthy kissing scenes by having Cary Grant and Ingrid Bergman shower one another with lots of quick kisses for longer than the appointed time. The mogul Howard Hughes openly defied the Code with *The Outlaw* in 1941, touring the United States with an uncut version of his film when the MPAA refused to release it.

By the end of World War II, it was clear that the Code's time was up. Men returning from the battlefield were in no mood to be babied by Hollywood, and audiences could see international films with much more daring content in independent cinemas after the 1948 Paramount Decree. In 1952, the Supreme Court overruled their earlier decision in the so-called Miracle case (related to Roberto Rossellini's 1948 *The*

The Code and women

It has been argued, by critics Molly Haskell and David Denby among others, that women actually benefitted from the Production Code. With the moral police banning characters such as the hooker with a heart of gold or the golddigger, Code-era screenwriters were often forced to turn their female characters into career gals in order to justify them spending time with their male heroes, and to rely on suggestive repartee rather than skimpy costumes to entertain audiences. In support of this argument, consider the female characters of the New Hollywood after the Code fell apart: a time when sex workers were once again overrepresented and women were more frequently naked or topless onscreen.

Miracle), and recognized that free speech rights applied to cinema, removing the threat of censorship. The MPAA had already stopped enforcing some of the stricter rules on dress, dancing and violence, but after that the move towards the rating system that exists today was inevitable. In 1968, at the start of what would be a long term atop the MPAA, Jack Valenti introduced an age-based ratings system that offered a little more flexibility for daring subject matter and storytelling.

Still, echoes of the Code remain. LGBTQI+ sex, and even kissing, is still more likely to result in a restrictive rating than equivalent heterosexual portrayals, and portrayals of female orgasm still result in a higher rating than depictions of male pleasure. Bad language is still, often, judged more harshly than violence, and honest depictions of sex more harshly than either. As far as the modern ratings system goes, it is gore but not bush even now.

> I believe in censorship. If a picture of mine didn't get an X rating, I'd be insulted
> Mae West

The condensed idea
A mandate on the stories that can and cannot be told

21 The New Hollywood

By the end of the 1960s, Hollywood was on its knees. High-budget, high-profile flops such as *Doctor Dolittle* (1967) and *Hello, Dolly!* (1969) had embarrassed the industry, while young audiences flocked to the new independent cinemas that offered more daring material from Europe, free of the long shadow of the Hays Code in Hollywood. Then, in 1967, Arthur Penn's *Bonnie and Clyde* won commercial and critical acclaim despite its violence and nihilism, shaking the old myths about what worked. Mike Nichols's *The Graduate*, released the same year, similarly seemed to tap into a sense of cynicism that had evaded the studios' notice. As a generation of aging studio heads retired, the new blood who replaced them tried to reach a youth audience.

The feeling was that new directors could talk to the soon-to-be-dominant baby boomer generation of filmgoers that the studios, evidently, could not. Relatively untried directors were therefore given the keys to the kingdom – or, at least, moderately sized budgets and a modicum of artistic freedom. The decade or so that followed saw an explosion of daring new American filmmakers.

The glory days

The result, initially, was extremely promising. Dennis Hopper's *Easy Rider* in 1969 was a major success, taking $60m on a $400,000 budget – despite a sometimes chaotic, drink-and-drug powered cross-country shoot. Some of the films that followed were also huge critical and commercial hits, such as 1972's *The Godfather* from Francis Ford Coppola. The studio thought Marlon Brando was too old and too fat; that Gordon Willis's striking chiaroscuro cinematography was too dark; that there was too much violence. Coppola, however, held off all their complaints and proved to have his finger on the pulse of America, to the tune of nearly $300m worldwide and three Oscars, including Best Picture.

Martin Scorsese, Brian De Palma, Peter Bogdanovich and many others who followed had studied classic Hollywood but also learned from the French New Wave and its successors. Given their chance, they did not want to perpetuate the system but to challenge it. The

Production Code was gone so these new films had sex, drugs, violence and dark, downbeat endings. Right did not always triumph, and good was rarely pure.

Films like *Coming Home* and *The Deer Hunter*, both 1978, touched directly on the fallout of the Vietnam War, but for many of the rest it was a bubbling undercurrent of discontent, mistrust of authority and a questioning of what, exactly, America was. Many of these films and filmmakers rejected the traditional Hollywood ending as overly pat, so you get the ambiguous finish of *The Graduate* and the hanging horror of *Rosemary's Baby* (1968). The storytelling style of *Easy Rider*, or any of Robert Altman's films of the time, was looser and less structured than most American films, while the understated, performance-focused style of Hal Ashby was a world away from the razzle-dazzle of 60s Hollywood. Scorsese's examination of masculinity, street life and Catholic guilt are far tougher edged than even most noir films. And the most old Hollywood of the bunch, Peter Bogdanovich,

Francis Ford Coppola

One of the most important directors of the New Hollywood, Coppola made his name as the Oscar-nominated cowriter of *Patton* in 1970, and as a result was offered a script he considered 'pretty cheap stuff': *The Godfather*. He turned it into a sprawling, three-hour crime epic that made more than $250m on a $9m budget and won three Oscars. He followed with two more masterpieces in one year, 1974's *The Conversation* and *The Godfather Part II*, but his next epic, 1979's *Apocalypse Now*, went wildly overbudget and caused Coppola a heart attack before emerging as his fourth classic. After that he struggled to make a bona fide hit, with his musical fantasy *One From The Heart* (1981) driving him to bankruptcy and leaving him a gun for hire for most of the next decade. Still, there is no arguing with his lasting influence.

who made the Dust Bowl *Paper Moon* (1973) still injected a little nip of modernity – one subplot in the screwball *What's Up Doc?* (1972) concerns government corruption.

The end of an era

A number of factors changed the game. Vast budget overruns on films such as Scorsese's *New York, New York* (1977) and Coppola's *Apocalypse Now* (1979) and flops like *Heaven's Gate* (1980) called into question the relative creative freedom that the early New Hollywood filmmakers had enjoyed. Perhaps even more significantly, two younger members of the set sometimes described as the Movie Brats (which included Coppola, Scorsese and De Palma), Steven Spielberg, with *Jaws* in 1975, and George Lucas, with *Star Wars* in 1977, showed that there were even bigger box-office prizes to be won by speaking not just to young adults with a taste for violence, but to people of all ages. The result was arguably a retreat to old Hollywood preoccupations and, to some extent, morality, but with new, more daring filmmaking technique and a more inventive style.

> We just gravitated towards these characters and these stories. When I was making them, I felt I should be there, rather than being hired and finding yourself in a place where you don't want to be.
> Martin Scorsese,
> *The Guardian*, 2024

Still, the influence of the New Hollywood persisted because it showed that originality and daring were possible in the studio system, and opened Hollywood's doors to darker, sexier and bloodier subjects than ever before. It swept away some of the lingering influence of the Production Code and inspired many filmmakers of the 80s and 90s who would go on to keep the independent spirit alive. It launched the careers of Scorsese, Coppola and many more, as well as stars such as Al Pacino, Robert De Niro and Jodie Foster. More widely, it was an influence on France's Cinéma du look and Italy's Poliziotteschi films; filmmakers like Hong Kong's John Woo also responded to some of these films and shaped their own responses.

It is notable who was *not* given the keys to the kingdom during the New Hollywood free-for-all. Female filmmakers like Juleen Compton, whose first two independent movies had screened at Cannes, and Shirley Clarke, who had screened at Cannes and Venice, found Hollywood closed. Maya Angelou attempted to make her first film in 1972 from her own screenplay, *Georgia, Georgia*, but despite studying cinematography ahead of the production, was not able to land the job, saying that 'in film, racism and sexism stand at the door' (she would finally make her first film in 1996, *Down in the Delta*). Female directors who did get to make a film, such as Elaine May, faced an uphill battle against studio interference and tended to be one flop away from the end of their career.

The condensed idea
Younger and more daring filmmakers reinvent US cinema

22 High concept

Two of the younger 'movie brats', Steven Spielberg and George Lucas, made films in the 1970s that would change the face of cinema. Spielberg's *Jaws*, in 1975, popularized the term 'blockbuster' to refer to a film that was a huge box-office hit, taking $476m on a $9m budget. Two years later, Lucas' *Star Wars* made $775m. These fundamentally changed cinema: studios started to look for films that would sell around the world and stay in cinemas for months at a time. The result was the 1980s and 1990s focus on 'high-concept' movies – original and memorable film ideas that could be stated in a sentence or less, brought to life with a big star name or two and spectacular action scenes.

The ability to recognize a big idea, and translate it, therefore became paramount, and superstar producers, directors and even screenwriters emerged, noted for their hit-making talents. The likes of Spielberg (as a producer as well as director), producers Don Simpson and Jerry Bruckheimer (*Beverly Hills Cop*; 1984) and James Cameron (*The Terminator*; 1984) built their careers, while screenwriters like Joe Eszterhas (*Flashdance*; 1983) and Shane Black (*Lethal Weapon*; 1987) earned record paydays. Not every film of the 1980s and 1990s was a high-concept hit, but the films that were dominated the decade: *Indiana Jones* and *E.T. The Extra-Terrestrial*, *Star Wars* sequels and *Top Gun*, *Back to the Future* and *Batman*. These were films with a clear and original idea (what if a teenager travelled back in time to his parents' youth? What if an alien befriended a kid?) but also with smart, stylish execution.

High concept vs the B-movie

These films were distinct from what had gone before because, unlike the 'low-concept' cinema of the 1970s, they were not necessarily concerned with character or thematic development, but with a simple premise, thrillingly explored. They were high-budget, slickly made films distinct from the 1950s B-movies that often shared similar snappy ideas (*Attack of the 50 Foot Woman*, say) or indeed the later low-budget likes of *Snakes on a Plane* (2006) or *Sharknado* (2013). There, too, the idea may be summed up in its entirety by the title, but the high-concept films are (at least arguably) distinguished by high production values and smart execution. This model of filmmaking appealed to studios because these ideas were easily grasped by everyone involved in making the film, easily marketed around the world, and often easy to build franchises or sequels upon. Numerous filmmakers have told stories of executives unwilling to consider any film that could not be described in a single sentence, while those best able to sell their ideas (James Cameron's legendary pitch for 1986's *Aliens*, where he marched in and wrote "Alien" on the back of a script and then added a dollar sign) flourished.

The look, hook and book

High-concept films were defined, by communications professor Jason Wyatt, by their 'look, hook and book'. The 'look' is the visual appeal of the film in marketing; think E.T.'s glowing finger or the dinosaurs in *Jurassic Park* (1993). There is often a single, stunning image on the poster or in the trailer that virtually demands that audiences head to cinemas to find out more – the shot of the boat turning vertical in

Titanic (1997) or the onrushing ghost in *Ghostbusters* (1984). The 'hook' is the intriguing idea – What if robots turned on us? What if you could trap ghosts? And the 'book' is all the sequel opportunities, tie-in merchandise and ancillary money that can be made from a film. This was a category that had been extant but underexplored in previous decades, but George Lucas's deal to hold merchandising rights to *Star Wars* had earned him tens of millions of dollars and shown that tie-in toys, clothing, lunchboxes and trade partnerships could have phenomenal value.

Not all high-concept movies were quite so broad in their appeal. The older-skewing, R-rated action movies of the 1980s also fall mostly into the category. In some cases, the high-concept there was essentially 'Arnold Schwarzenegger (or Sylvester Stallone, or a little later Jean-Claude Van Damme) takes on an army of baddies' with little further embroidery. These muscle-bound heroes told largely uncomplicated

Steven Spielberg

A product of the New Hollywood, Steven Spielberg came into filmmaking with a veneration of the French New Wave and Golden Age of Hollywood and an astonishing grasp of what great movie entertainment involved. He turned pulp fiction into blockbusters such as *Jaws* and *Jurassic Park*, and old 1930s serial adventures into the Indiana Jones franchise. As a producer, he shepherded the likes of *Back to the Future* (1985), *The Goonies* (1985) and *Who Framed Roger Rabbit* (1988) to success. Probably no one (with the arguable exception of James Cameron) has a better grasp of how to make high-concept films, and the impact of *Jaws* (1975), *Close Encounters of the Third Kind* (1977), *Raiders of the Lost Ark* (1981) and *E.T. The Extra-Terrestrial* (1982) fundamentally changed Hollywood's expectations of how much a film could make (alongside *Star Wars*). However, Spielberg himself has warned against over-reliance on huge-budget films, and has continued to make smaller and 'low-concept' such as *Schindler's List* (1993), *Lincoln* (2012) and *The Fabelmans* (2022) alongside his bigger releases.

stories of good vs evil and might making right, perhaps in keeping with the muscular patriotism of the Reagan years in the United States. The term was most common in blockbuster cinema – that is, high-budget action or adventure movies for the summer or Christmas season. However, the term has been used to describe films where the premise is simply summed up, as in *Liar Liar* (1997) or *Elf* (2003) and romcoms like *My Best Friend's Wedding* (1997) and *Serendipity* (2001). It also exists outside Hollywood: a good way to spot if a foreign film is "high concept" is that Hollywood has remade it...or tried to. *Taxi* (1998), *Battle Royale* (2000) and *Infernal Affairs* (2002) all have impeccably high concepts.

For film critics and theorists, the essential shallowness of the high-concept approach means that it is of limited appeal, precisely because of the almost built-in lack of character nuance and human complication in most high-concept cinema, but even many critics will admit that the best high-concept films can be thrilling to watch. Almost all Christopher Nolan films, for example, are high concepts. At the time of writing, we are still in a high-concept world, because it is now baked into the fabric of what we expect from the biggest films.

The condensed idea
A reason to watch, summed up in a single sentence

23 The indie era

Perhaps in reaction to the Hollywood studios' fixation with blockbuster filmmaking in the 1980s, an alternative American cinema began to grow through the late 1980s, and especially with the dawn of the 1990s. Inspired by foreign filmmakers they saw doing more transgressive, daring work, by the examples of the New Hollywood of the 60s and 70s and, in some cases, by the low-budget grindhouse that flourished outside mainstream Hollywood, these new, independent filmmakers sought to inject a little Generation X edge into their movies.

The centre of this movement was the Sundance Film Festival, established in 1978 as the Utah/US Film Festival to showcase American-made films outside the studio system. Renamed in 1991 after Robert Redford's cowboy character (with Redford's blessing), the Festival provided breakthrough support for filmmakers that included Steven Soderbergh, Quentin Tarantino, Kevin Smith, Paul Thomas Anderson, Jim Jarmusch and Alison Anders.

Richard Linklater

The most prolific Sundance filmmaker, and one of the most successful, is Richard Linklater, who first went to the Festival with his second film, 1990's *Slacker*, and has returned seven more times. That film, and follow-ups including *Dazed & Confused* (1993) and *Before Sunrise* (1995), summed up the Gen X energy of the independent film generation, while his Oscar-winning coming-of-age drama *Boyhood* (2014) was a daring experimental triumph, filmed for a few days at a time every year for more than a decade. Typically, his films are less about plot than about people, and while he has made hit studio films like *School of Rock* (2003), he remains a largely independent film producer with his own Texas base.

The films that played at Sundance that year [1991] were to start an explosion of American independent cinema. . .It was a bit like being a rock star. Young people in college were following them and all of a sudden now it wasn't music performers that they had on their wall. It was like the poster from the independent movie that they liked.

Quentin Tarantino, *W Magazine*'s Five Things with Lynn Hirschberg podcast

The independent breakthroughs

Soderbergh's *sex, lies, and videotape* (1989) is generally considered to have fired the starting gun for the whole movement. Made for just $1.2m, it took over $36m worldwide at the box office and was a hit on home video. More to the point, Soderbergh won the Palme d'Or at Cannes at the age of just 26, dominated the fairly new Independent Spirit Awards and picked up Golden Globe and Oscar nominations. The film's success was evidence that independent filmmakers could connect with audiences on a large scale, and small distributors began to search for new, low-budget films to build on the trend.

Independent cinema's real *Star Wars* moment came a few years later, however. Quentin Tarantino's first film, *Reservoir Dogs* (1992), had been a modest box-office success but had earned newspaper column inches, awards attention and critical buzz as well as controversy, and enough of a reputation that his second film was eagerly awaited. That film, 1994's *Pulp Fiction*, made more than $200m worldwide on an $8m budget, winning not only the Palme d'Or but also Best Screenplay at the Oscars (its Best Picture loss to Robert Zemeckis' *Forrest Gump* is often described now as an Oscar mistake). With a cast that included Bruce Willis, it showed that independent film could offer A-list stars a chance to do more daring, more critically acclaimed work, and its long legs on VHS and later DVD showed that indie film was no passing phase.

A brave new world?

Many of the same prejudices ruled those early years: queer themes were still seen as both risky and risqué; non-male and non-white directors still struggled to break through. With the exception of Spike Lee, who won a Student Academy Award while still in college, Black directors of the 1980s and 1990s like Matty Rich (*Straight Out of*

Brooklyn; 1991) and Julie Dash (*Daughters of the Dust*; 1991) struggled for the chance to follow up their indie debuts with studio work, either denied any offers of more work or micromanaged into oblivion. If Sundance's early years had been dominated by talky tragedies, the 90s would see it swamped with Tarantino wannabes making crime dramas. However, it did inject a sense of energy into American film and challenged both the small-c and big-C conservatism of 1980s filmmaking. As the 90s progressed and more and more filmmakers emerged from the indie scene to commercial or critical acclaim, Hollywood moved slightly to meet the demand for more original, daring stories, to generally good effect.

As Sundance – and other, similar festivals – became more known as incubators of talent and potential hits, the money involved has climbed. During a streaming service-fuelled boom in acquisitions by the early 2020s, Apple TV bought the rights to *CODA* for $25m – which paid off with a win for Best Picture and almost a million household views in the United States.

Some indie filmmakers transitioned to making studio pictures or proceeded on a Soderbergh style 'one for them, one for me' approach to their work. Some of those directors have kept their own sensibility entirely intact in the studio arena – Tarantino or Paul Thomas Anderson, for example – or found a way to smuggle their own priorities into studio filmmaking – Ryan Coogler or Lee Isaac Chung. Others have apparently grasped at the opportunities of the mainstream without hesitation, leaving their counter-culture roots more or less behind to embrace huge scale storytelling.

A permanent shift

The indie era did, however, establish that independent films could have financial muscle, something that had not always been clear to Hollywood. While Roger Corman, for example, maintained an eight-decade, 500-odd film career as an independent producer, his micro-budgeted films had been more or less an aside to the Hollywood juggernaut. Tarantino and Michael Moore were another matter, proving that independently made films could be vastly more profitable than the majority of Hollywood's own output.

Independent film also succeeded in launching numerous subgenres, from mumblecore to torture porn to found footage. Some of these became major hits when picked up and marketed properly – consider *The Blair Witch Project* in 1999 or *Saw* in 2004 – and this, in turn, lays the groundwork for further experimentation and more breakthroughs for new filmmakers.

The condensed idea
Fresh filmmaking talent that challenged Hollywood

24 Film franchises

We tend to think of film as single, stand-alone stories, in contrast to episodic television shows. However, since almost the dawn of cinema, there have been film franchises, series following beloved characters or concepts through multiple films. The *Mr & Mrs Jones* (1908) comedy shorts were one early example, and were followed by *The Keystone Cops* (1912–17) movies from Mack Sennett. The studio attitude was always that, if the people like something, give them more of it.

For a very long time, franchises were only a small part of Hollywood's output, and many of them could only be loosely so defined. The films of Charlie Chaplin or Laurel and Hardy sometimes shared a central character, such as the Little Tramp, and perhaps a catchphrase or concept, but they were rarely linked in narrative terms. Wives and girlfriends in Laurel and Hardy came and went, and there was little to no continuing story. The common link was a character – and not necessarily a human one: *Rin Tin Tin* and *Lassie* movies were hugely successful. A little later in the studio era, MGM's Mickey Rooney-starring *Andy Hardy* films showed that a loose continuing story might be popular, and the popularity of radio and screen serials at the time bled a little into Hollywood.

Following the example of *The Godfather* (1972) and *Jaws* (1975), the franchise became the default mode of big-budget movie making in the 1980s and has remained so. It was once received wisdom that sequels made less than their predecessor, but the sequels to *Star Wars* (1977) and *Raiders of The Lost Ark* (1981) narrowed that gap, and studios concluded that the money saved in awareness-building more-or-less offset the slightly reduced upfront box office.

In the late 1990s and early 2000s, this tendency became particularly pronounced. A 'tentpole' model of releases grew in Hollywood, and spread to much of the rest of the cinematic world. This decreed that a small number of big-budget, heavily advertised films would serve as 'tentpoles' in the studio's annual calendar, released on popular filmgoing weekends and aiming for record box-office numbers. Leaders such as Alan Horn at Warner Bros leaned into a new theory of business that said, counterintuitively, that it is more lucrative to

Shared universes

A shared universe is a sort of meta-franchise, where characters with their own hit films can cross paths or team up in a common adventure. The most famous early example is the *Universal Monster* series, which saw Dracula, Frankenstein's monster and the Wolfman cross paths at various points. Toho's Godzilla and its Western cousin, the Monsterverse, are both shared universes, as technically are many of Quentin Tarantino's films. The successful *Alien* and *Predator* franchises crossed over with the *Alien Vs Predator* franchise in the early 2000s, and Blumhouse's *The Conjuring* series has launched so many sub-series that it qualifies as a shared universe now. By some distance the most famous shared universe, however, is the Marvel Cinematic Universe or MCU, with more than 30 films and over $30bn at the global box office. Launched with 2008's *Iron Man*, the MCU debuted four sub-franchises (*Iron Man, The Incredible Hulk, Thor, Captain America*) before teaming them all up in 2012's *Avengers*. That film's $1.5bn box office showed that the gamble, of mimicking the comic-book crossovers and event covers of the source material, had thoroughly paid off.

invest heavily in a small number of blockbuster efforts than to spread risk and reward across a larger number of more modestly budgeted releases. Filmmakers like Steven Spielberg and George Lucas warned that the strategy could topple studios, because only a few films needed to significantly underperform to threaten the entire bottom line, but the soaring profits at Warner Bros and, later, Disney suggested that the strategy was not just tenable but essential.

So, Hollywood reached a situation in the late 2010s and early 2020s where most of the top films each year are franchise instalments – or are themselves envisioned as the launching point for a new franchise. Older films that still had name-brand recognition, but whose stars were unable or unwilling to return, were remade and, when that phrase lost its appeal to audiences, 'rebooted' for a new generation and for a new series of planned sequels. The reboot was dominant in the early 2000s, but faded after the commercial and critical failure of the new *Robocop*, *Total Recall* and *Point Break*, to name but a few. Instead, new franchises and shared universes (see box-out) took hold and became hugely important.

This is not a sign that filmmakers have lost all creativity and daring, though it is arguably a sign that that may be true for studios. It is more an acknowledgement of the economic realities of modern filmmaking. Now that studios are trying to sell their films around the world, they need widely recognized and recognizable names, and there are very few movie stars able to open to huge box office around the world on the strength of only their own name. Franchises, perhaps based on existing brands (for example, *Barbie*) or intellectual property (*Resident Evil*) that had already spread around the world, offered an easy way to guarantee interest across a huge percentage of the globe.

The canon

Each franchise, even the most loosely connected, has a 'canon', an internal story that forms the spine of the continuing saga. A key issue to decide with each new film, and in particular with any reboots or re-quels (a sequel that is also a sort of reboot) is to decide what carries over. The Bond films, for example, have sometimes changed the Bond star without rotating his supporting cast, and audiences might wonder if they are all the same guy or different agents operating under the same name (likely the former). When the canon becomes unwieldy or the history too dense, the entire series may be rebooted (which definitely happened with Bond in *Casino Royale* (2006) which saw him starting out as a 00-agent) or certain films may be jettisoned (*Superman Returns* (2006) continued from *Superman II* (1980), ignoring *Superman III* and *IV* (1983 and 1987)). Supplementary media can also be similarly jettisoned: all *Star Wars* films, books and cartoons outside the central six films and *Clone Wars* were de-canonized in 2014. Any very long-running series tends to develop canon problems eventually due to the sheer weight of storytelling, but at the same time audiences expect the stories they already love to matter.

The condensed idea
Films stand alone – but can be profitable when they do not

25 #MeToo

In October 2017, an article by Megan Twohey and Jodi Kantor in the *New York Times* published allegations of sexual harassment by film producer Harvey Weinstein. A few days later, an investigation by Ronan Farrow in *The New Yorker* made significant additional claims against the mini-mogul. Celebrities and many everyday women, led by Alyssa Milano, adopted the #MeToo social media hashtag first used by activist Tarana Burke to express their support for the accusers, and to chronicle their own experiences of harassment and sexual assault. This exploded across traditional media as more and more people – especially, but not only, in Hollywood – spoke about sexual predation. It became known as the #MeToo movement.

Harvey Weinstein

Weinstein was at the centre of the first accusations, with more than 80 women naming him and a criminal case launched against him in New York in 2018. In 2020 he was convicted on two felony counts, but his conviction was overturned in 2024 and sent for retrial. He was also

Men, women and children

The #MeToo movement was not only about women. Men, including Anthony Rapp, Brendan Fraser, Terry Crews and James Van Der Beek spoke out about their experiences of sexual harassment in Hollywood. Muscles and physical size did not protect them because their predators trusted in their own status to give them all the leverage they needed to do whatever they wanted. Child stars such as Corey Feldman also had their concerns about the abuse of child actors taken more seriously than ever before as a result of the #MeToo energy, with Eliza Dushku, for example, speaking about an assault she suffered aged just 12.

convicted of three charges in California and sentenced in 2023 to 16 years in prison.

The harassment described by Weinstein victims was consistent across multiple accounts and many years. Actresses and assistants reported being called to meetings in hotel rooms, only to be faced with a semi-nude producer, demands for a massage, or sexual assault and rape. His accusers said that Weinstein implied, sometimes promised, professional opportunities in return for sexual compliance, and that his reputation as not only a successful film producer, but a seasoned Oscar campaigner, gave his inducements weight even when he did not resort to physical threats.

> Any industry that has that much power and is that competitive. . .there's always going to be somebody willing to take abuse and stay quiet.
> Evan Rachel Wood, in the documentary *Showbiz Kids*

Why Hollywood?

The #MeToo campaign, however, was not about one man. It was a largely spontaneous, rolling movement that spoke out against a long-standing problem in Hollywood (and more widely in other industries, and in countries around the world), which was the sexually predatory attitude of a mostly male group in positions of power or influence over the usually younger and less powerful hoping to progress in their careers. Hollywood was a particularly fertile hunting ground because of the ad-hoc nature of casting and hiring processes, lack of oversight and immense power differentials between the would-be stars and assistants on one hand, and the agents, producers and executives who held the keys to the kingdom on the other.

Stories of the 'casting couch' – of demands for sexual favours in return for roles – pre-date Hollywood, of course. The term originated on Broadway, but the practice goes back far further under any number of epithets. Such stories sprang up in Hollywood almost from the day that it became the centre of the US film industry. Stars of the past, including Joan Crawford, Marilyn Monroe and Dorothy Dandridge, reported what we would now call sexual harassment by producers and studio bosses; certain executives such as Harry Cohn were notorious predators. The casting couch was whispered about and joked about (usually at the expense of the women or young men involved rather than the culprits) but no one seriously thought it could be eradicated.

One practical response to the #MeToo movement, albeit one not directly connected to its central allegations, is the soaring demand for intimacy coordinators on film sets. These experts help to choreograph and manage sex scenes and any other intimate contact, liaising between actors and directors or executives to ensure that no one is being made to do anything they are uncomfortable with, while also ensuring the best possible outcome for the look of the scene. This helps young actors maintain boundaries without, hopefully, incurring the wrath of powerful producers who might damage their careers, and ensures everyone's mental and emotional safety in the same way that a stunt coordinator might ensure their physical safety.

When people *had* spoken up they had usually been silenced by intimidation, pay outs or a mixture of both. Most lost their careers as a result. Court conviction rates in cases of harassment, sexual assault or rape lacking overwhelming physical evidence were almost zero, so being bought off at the cost of a non-disclosure agreement (NDA) was generally the least worst option for complainants of bad behaviour. This rarely included any admission of liability and does not seem to have much affected the careers of the accused nor, necessarily, their predations. Twohey and Kantor, for example, reported that Weinstein had made at least eight settlements to actresses, assistants, temps and others to secure their silence, but this had apparently led to no serious attempt, by Weinstein or anyone with significant influence on him, to change his behaviour.

The aftermath

The explosion of #MeToo testimony that followed those initial reports, and the stalwart support of voices that included Rose McGowan, Ashley Judd, Alyssa Milano, Lupita Nyong'o, Salma Hayek and Annabella Sciorra, among others, shifted the public understanding of what harassment is and how it persists. Discussions began about ways to improve the situation, with many companies putting systems in place that should pick up patterns of abuse, and calls for the reduction or regulation of NDAs. In the immediate aftermath of the movement, some 200 men lost their jobs, and just over half were replaced by women. Many companies made serious efforts to diversify their power structures, so there would be no 'boy's club' to cover for harassers, and introduced safeguards to reduce the opportunity for abuse.

Much of the talk fell away without any concrete action, and many responsible for harassment remain uninvestigated and unpunished. However, the #MeToo moment was significant for Hollywood in marking a psychological shift in attitudes. No longer can predators be relatively certain of impunity and anonymity; no longer do women fear to speak even to one another about abuse. Another such moment could occur, and the powerful and predatory must now consider the consequences of their actions in a way they never had to before.

The condensed idea
A moment when survivors challenged the power balance in Hollywood – and worldwide

26 German Expressionism

A highly stylized, primarily artistic movement from Germany in the late 1910s and early 1920s, German Expressionism was popularized at home amid the darkness of World War I but found huge success abroad when the war ended. It travelled around the world not only on the strength of its own exemplars, but also through a generation of emigre German and German-trained directors who took their ideas with them when they left its borders.

The Expressionist movement

The Expressionists rejected, both intellectually and practically, the imprecision of Impressionism, but also the dullness of naturalism. The movement's big idea was to turn from realism in favour of representing some internal truth, and using the images onscreen – costumes, make-up, sets and performance – to communicate emotion or vision, first and foremost. This was of a piece with the wider art movement of modernism, which also emphasized subjectivity and abstraction, and which rejected tradition in search of some new way of life. The seismic shifts of the 19th century, with agrarian countries becoming industrial, had led to what was seen as dehumanization, and an emphasis on subjectivity was a way of moving power back into the hands of the individual.

Expressionism in cinema

Expressionism found a natural home in cinema, where silence prevented the full replication of reality at the time, and where black-and-white film lent itself to striking, stark imagery. Germany was also receptive to new, experimental forms because an embargo on foreign films during World War I, and the collapse of local exports, had created a small but wildly productive local industry. Yearly production more than quintupled during the war, and that productivity supported a certain amount of experimentation with new ideas and new ways of working. It also meant that when men like Fritz Lang and F W Murnau left the army following tough wartime experiences, they could approach dark and difficult subjects and find their nation alongside them.

So, by 1920, the first masterpieces of Expressionism were emerging. Robert Wiene's *The Cabinet of Dr Caligari* (1920) was a tale of insanity, brainwashing and murder, but it is most famed for its disturbing look. The team of Hermann Warm (mostly sets), Walter Röhrig (mostly paintings) and Walter Reimann (mostly costumes) created a space of unnatural angles and twisted perspective. There are sharp points, oblique lines, spirals and curves, with an almost Cubist-style approach to the architecture. The acting, too, is over-emphasized, less about nature than exaggeration, while the occasional sudden close-up creates a sense of shock. In the same year, *From Morn to Midnight* emerged from Karlheinz Martin in an even more stylized form. There, sets were painted in rough, almost child-like lines on dark backgrounds, and everyday characters transformed into Death at a glance.

> Our whole effort must be bent toward ridding motion pictures of *all that does not belong to them*, of all that is unnecessary and trivial and drawn from other sources – all the tricks, gags, 'business' not of the cinema, but of the stage, and the written book.
> F W Murnau interview, 1926

During the next decade or so, Expressionism produced such masterpieces as *Nosferatu* (1922), *Metropolis* (1927), *The Blue Angel* (1930) and *M* (1931). Some of the wild experimentation of its early days died down in those later films, which have more conventional sets and performances, but the Expressionist influence remains strong in its rejection of strict realism and emphasis on emotional impact. However, shifts in German politics proved difficult to survive. The hyperinflation and political upheavals of the Weimar years made for a difficult export market for films, and the Nazi party made life dangerous for the openly anti-fascist Lang, for example, who also had Jewish heritage. Some scholars, including Lotte Eisner in *The Haunted Screen* (1952), have seen a link between Expressionism and the rise of Hitler, with the romanticism of its early days giving way to dark and totalitarian visions in later Expressionist films (think of the toiling hordes in Fritz Lang's *Metropolis*). However, the exodus of many of the movement's leading lights suggests that it was never the intention of most Expressionists to support Nazism.

Nosferatu

F W Murnau's 1922 attempt to tell a Dracula story without securing the rights to Bram Stoker's book did not escape the copyright lawyers, but it became a classic in its own right. Max Schreck plays Count Orlof, the film's Dracula figure, who brings a plague to the German town he visits when he leaves his remote home, and seeks to prey on the lawyer who helped him and the lawyer's wife. The film's Expressionist roots are evident in the looming shadow of the vampire rising up the stairs, and in Schreck's unforgettable make-up and performance. The first story in which the sun was fatal to vampires, this has been directly remade three times and is influential on the entire horror genre.

Lasting legacy

Expressionism was hugely influential in American horror filmmaking, and had a major impact on the chiaroscuro lighting of film noir. That is partly because these films were striking and popular, and many directors attempted to mimic their look. But it is also because many German filmmakers either moved to Hollywood for the money or fled there after the rise of the Nazis in the 1930s. Some such emigres found enormous success and carried elements of the style into their studio work. That included not only Lang, who made noir milestones there such as *Scarlet Street* (1945) and *The Big Heat* (1953), but also the likes of cinematographer Karl Freund, who shot *Metropolis* for Lang before shooting *Dracula* for Universal in 1931 and directing *The Mummy* the following year, directly importing the Expressionist style into American horror. Then there was Expressionist acolyte Alfred Hitchcock, who worked at Babelsberg Studios in Potsdam as a young director in 1924, and was influenced by Expressionism for the rest of his long career.

Expressionism survives today both directly, in remakes such as Robert Eggers' 2025 *Nosferatu*, and indirectly in its stylistic influence, seen in sci-fi (*Blade Runner*; 1982 and *Dark City*; 1998), in almost every Tim Burton fantasy (*Sleepy Hollow*; 1999 and *Batman Returns*; 1992) and some Yorgos Lanthimos performances; in Darren Aronofsky's *Pi* (1998) and David Lynch's *The Elephant Man* (1980). Its basic ideas opened film up to more daring and evocative techniques.

The condensed idea
Bold design and exaggerated performances that communicate a deeper, emotional truth

27 Surrealism

Most art, to some extent at least, attempts to mirror reality. Surrealism takes reality as a starting point only to reject or subvert it, basing its work in the unconscious rather than the world outside one's mind. It is important to cinema because it was perhaps the first 'serious' wider art movement to embrace film as part of its means of expression, based in cinema just as much as fine art and literature. As the Surrealists started work in the 1920s, only just after cinema had become a popular art form, they quickly saw its power and possibility, producing Surrealist film scenes and short films soon after André Breton's Surrealist manifesto was published in 1924.

Surrealism owed much to the 'anti-art' and Dadaist movements that preceded it, and certain works, such as René Clair's *Entr'acte*, in 1924, have been attributed to both. Dadaism uses nonsense and illogic to protest war and capitalism, overlapping with Surrealism's attempts to communicate a deeper truth of the mind by what the first Surrealist manifesto defined as 'psychic automatism', an attempt to communicate the process of thought itself with no attempt to impose reason or beauty upon the results.

Apollinaire and Freud

Many of Surrealism's early figures were admirers of Guillaume Apollinaire, the French poet who had contributed to Cubism (he coined both that word and 'surrealism') and who advocated for abstract art when it faced popular scorn. Apollinaire rejected traditional rules in his own writing and in his art criticism, and championed work that came directly from the imagination without attempting to appeal to traditional sensibilities. The author Michael Robinson defined Surrealism as 'an activity with broadening horizons' rather than a style or a particular concept in itself – a question of interconnected concepts rather than a set of images from which meaning could be individually derived.

As with many artistic movements of the 20th century, Surrealism was indebted to psychoanalysis and played with the dream symbolism of Sigmund Freud. Breton's initial manifesto (he would write two more, while Yvan Goll would write a rival one) identified both the dream state and the hypnagogic, nearly asleep state as Surrealist territory and a source of inspiration. The Surrealists saw cinema itself as a similar not-quite-real form, a way to stop short of faithfully representing reality and even transform it. However, it is worth noting that the melting clocks, strange beasts and lobster-shaped apparel and accessories that many associate with Surrealism are not necessary or sufficient to describe the movement. An attempt to depict dream logic is not the only way to create Surrealist art; it may also be done by channelling the subconscious in ways that appear closer to reality. Some of the more horrifying images of the Surrealist movement draw from the disasters of World War I, with the trauma of a generation reflected in the deliberately jarring, shocking ideas put onscreen.

Pure Surrealism

There are few purely Surrealist films and the term has been applied to films that only partially fit the bill. Elements of the approach can be found in the dream sequences of Jean Renoir's 1925 film *The Whirlpool of Fate*, and in the near-death experiences of 1928's *The Fall of the*

Absurdism

Absurdism, and the Theatre of the Absurd, emerged around the same time as Surrealism, after the horrors of World War I, though it was inspired by early philosophical work by Søren Kierkegaard and Immanuel Kant. It also owed a debt to Dadaism and anti-art, and frequently featured counter-reality images and bizarre narrative turns. However, where Surrealism tried to pack meaning into every element it uses, Absurdism celebrated a total lack of meaning. It remains an existential and sometimes nihilistic form, but it gives a bittersweet edge to work by filmmakers such as the Coen Brothers, the Daniels, Yorgos Lanthimos and Werner Herzog.

House of Usher by Jean Epstein (no surprise, with Luis Buñuel assisting on the script). Luis Buñuel's 21-minute *Un Chien Andalou* (1929) is sometimes called the first completely Surrealist film, and his 60-minute *L'Age d'Or* (1930) made with the Spanish artist Salvador Dalí, is also considered a Surrealist milestone. The American artist Joseph Cornell also made films that are considered Surrealist, including *Rose Hobart* (1936), where he spliced together scenes from a 1931 B-movie called *East of Borneo* with nature documentaries. The Surrealist Man Ray is today best remembered for his photography, but he made films too, like *Les Mystères du Château du Dé* (1929), which explores chance and randomness.

There is considerable overlap between the Surrealists and the Dadaists, avant-garde and experimental film movements; some filmmakers and films have been claimed for multiple causes. All four, however, share a determination to question the mundane, challenge the status quo and decide upon their own rules when creating art.

Legacy

Surrealist film proved more influential in bits and pieces than in full feature films – lengthy periods of feeling unmoored from reality seems to be a niche taste. And just as it is usually boring to hear someone else's dreams recounted the next morning, it appears that audiences may not enjoy being fully immersed in someone else's subconscious for too long. Alfred Hitchcock would later call on Dalí to provide the dream sequences for his psychoanalysis thriller *Spellbound* in 1948. Dalí also worked with Walt Disney on an animated film, *Destino*, that was begun in 1945 but not finished until 2003, after Disney abandoned the project for lack of commercial appeal. Sure enough, Surrealism has largely remained a fringe activity that rarely has commercial appeal outside auction houses selling Dalí paintings or Elsa Schiaparelli designs, but it remains attractive. It has survived into the present day through the work of filmmakers like Joseph Cornell, Maya Deren, Jan Švankmajer, Alejandro Jodorowsky and even David Lynch or Charlie Kaufman.

> Buñuel always told me that the best thing was not to show things to the audience, but instead to trigger their imagination.
>
> Franco Nero, quoted in *Film Comment*

Luis Buñuel

The Spanish Surrealist Luis Buñuel formed a close friendship with the poet and playwright Federico García Lorca and the painter Salvador Dalí while at university in Madrid. He and Dalí then worked together on the 1929 short film *Un Chien Andalou*, which he hoped would shock even audiences accustomed to avant-garde work, but which instead proved successful and influential. After his Surrealist years, he developed his filmmaking career in Mexico before returning to France to become a critical darling at Cannes with films attacking Spanish fascism (*Viridiana*; 1961) and conventional morality (*Belle de Jour*; 1967).

The condensed idea
Channelling the unconscious mind directly to the screen

28 Italian neorealism

The Italian neorealist movement galvanized and transformed Italian cinema – and, arguably, much of later European and American cinema – in the aftermath of World War II and into the 1950s. Italy, which had entered the war as an Axis power, emerged from it defeated and economically devastated, with many of its industrial and cultural centres ravaged by the conflict and its population demoralized. Cinema's response was to face this crisis head on with a filmmaking style that looked unflinchingly at the population's woes and brought them to the screen with as little mediation as possible.

In terms of style, the movement was also a reaction to the Telefoni Bianchi (white telephone) films of the Mussolini years; light comedies that were shorn of all political and social commentary, leaning heavily on lavish sets and costumes to promote their conservative values and unchallenging comedy. These portrayed and promoted a comfortable, consumerist lifestyle – the white telephones that gave them their nickname were a status symbol – that was far from the reality of most

Bicycle Thieves

Vittorio Da Sica's 1948 *Bicycle Thieves* is one of the handful of films universally recognized as belonging to the neorealism movement, and near universally considered a masterpiece. It is the story of a man (Lamberto Maggiorani) who is offered a job he desperately needs on condition that he can provide his own bicycle. When it is stolen, he and his son (Enzo Staiola) go on a quest around Rome in an attempt to recover it. De Sica had to borrow money from friends to get the film made, using non-professional actors as his cast and public streets as his studio. It was met with hostility from Italian critics, who found it unduly negative, but embraced elsewhere around the world and awarded an honorary Oscar in 1950.

Italians at the time. In contrast, the neorealist films were shot for the most part on real streets and in real settings in an almost documentary style, with an emphasis on showing life as it was rather than how the government wished it to be. Many of its heroes were downtrodden or poverty stricken. They were often in opposition to the government or rejected by it. Some of neorealism's most extraordinary performances were given by non-professional actors, recruited for their understanding of the characters' plight.

The beginnings of neorealism

Luchino Visconti's 1943 film *Obsession* is sometimes described as the first neorealist film, but the movement's international debut is more often dated to the debut of Roberto Rossellini's *Rome, Open City* at the Cannes Film Festival in 1946. The story of a Resistance fighter trying to escape the Nazis in occupied Rome, it was set in run-down apartments and in jail cells rather than among the city's famous landmarks, though it finishes with a pointed shot of the dome of St Peter's over the city. In many neorealist films, characters were put in an impossible situation that gave the tension and urgency

[I had] to invent a new technique that allowed making films without using studios. This realism was simply born from the condition of work. Perhaps also from stubbornness.
Roberto Rossellini, 1974

necessary to drive the film forward, but without a traditionally unfolding plot to develop. The result was a more stripped down, and sometimes downbeat, air of overwhelming need.

As with the slightly later French New Wave, many of the men who would become leading lights of this Italian movement worked for a time as critics at the same magazine – in this case, *Cinema*. Visconti, Gianni Puccini, Cesare Zavattini, Giuseppe De Santis and Pietro Ingrao all worked there, and when their editor banned them from writing about politics in print (that editor was Vittorio Mussolini, the dictator's son) their leftist leanings found expression in film scripts and storytelling ideas that would burst forth with the fall of that regime. Their influences included the French filmmaker Jean Renoir, but also Hollywood: the last shot of *Bicycle Thieves* (1948), for example, was inspired by Charlie Chaplin.

The exact number of neorealist films made is still debated by critics and academics, but even the most generous definitions put the total of qualifying films at under 250 over a roughly ten-year period, and estimates go as low as 20. It was, in other words, never a majority movement in Italian film or at the box office, and many neorealist directors struggled even to raise the small budgets they required. As with the later, stripped-down approach of Dogme 95, the degree of adherence to strict neorealist principles varies from film to film, with some reliant on professional actors and moving away from the documentary style of the early films.

The economic miracle and decline

Remarkably quickly after the war, with the help of the US Marshall Plan, Italy began to recover from its economic malaise, and in 1957, it joined the new European Common Market. The doom and gloom of the neorealist films began to seem out of step with a new sense of optimism, and Italian critics and audiences turned away from this type of filmmaking in favour of something lighter. In artistic terms,

Federico Fellini

A giant of Italian cinema, and one of the most influential directors ever to step behind a camera, Federico Fellini got his start in film as a screenwriter. While much of his early work was comical, he wrote the screenplay to *Rome, Open City* with Roberto Rossellini, and collaborated with the director on several of his early neorealist efforts. Some of Fellini's own early films, like 1954's *La Strada* are generally considered transitional from neorealism to the more individualistic style that followed it, which had huge success in Fellini's own *La Dolce Vita* in 1960. Fellini himself went on to follow a more baroque, extravagant direction, with psychological exploration and even Surrealism influencing later films such as *81/2* (1963). Still, his films retained a certain earthiness that perhaps owes something to those neorealist roots.

the movement's focus on social crisis was replaced by more individualistic storytelling, with filmmakers such as Federico Fellini exploring the fragility of individual humans rather than a class or political struggle.

However, the movement's impact reverberated globally. Neorealistic films were lavished with praise at international film festivals, and had a major influence on other films around the world such as Nicholas Ray's noir *They Live By Night* (1948), Satyajit Ray's *Pather Panchali* (1955) and Tomás Gutiérrez Alea's *Memories of Underdevelopment* (1968). Neorealism offered a way to critically examine power structures, social disaffection and dystopia in the modern city, and its emphasis on desperation and struggle over traditional plot was easy to translate around the world.

The condensed idea
Emphasizing realism and naturalism to affect social change

29 French New Wave

Arguably the movement with the biggest impact on filmmaking in the second half of the 20th century, the French New Wave (Nouvelle Vague) was an artistic movement rebelling against certain traditions in French cinema that were already considered stale and trite by the young men at its heart, only 60 or so years after the creation of film itself. While it is hard to pinpoint a shared aesthetic or common theme in their work, what is undisputed is that there was a sort of 'youth quake', as music commentators would call the emergence of The Beatles a few years later, with a group of idealistic, mostly artistically minded, young filmmakers almost entirely displacing the old guard in a sudden generational shift.

The term 'new wave' was one applied by French newspapers to the entire generation of 20-somethings in the 1950s, not only these filmmakers, but it became remarkably appropriate to them. Their generation went to the cinema in huge numbers – accounting for about 43 per cent of attendees at Parisian cinemas in the 1950s. They

Agnès Varda

Born in Belgium but a French resident from her teenage years, Varda trained in art history and as a still photographer before making her first film in 1955, slightly prior to the birth of the New Wave. However, her first film, *La Pointe Courte* (1955), was a hit with the young Turks at *Cahiers*, not yet filmmakers, and her 1962 film *Cleo from 5 to 7* was a jewel of the movement. Varda sometimes struggled to get money for feature work, instead working on shorts, but she built documentary style and even still photos into her films, describing her style as 'cinematic writing', using all the elements of a film to communicate her message. Her final film, *Varda By Agnes*, came out in 2019, the same year she died at the age of 90. She is considered the godmother of the New Wave, and a significant figure in feminist film history.

were fanatical about film. As France was losing its empire and processing its new, post-war reality, these young voices started trying to change its rather moribund cinema (at least in their view). Just to put their impact in perspective, between 1945 and 1957, 20 per cent of French films were made by just nine directors. Between 1958 and 1962, 162 filmmakers made their first feature, according to a December 1962 edition of *Cahiers du cinéma*. It was a paradigm shift in filmmaking.

The young Turks

At the heart of the movement was a group referred to as the 'young Turks' that included Jean-Luc Godard, François Truffaut, Eric Rohmer, Jacques Rivette and Claude Chabrol. They had all worked as critics at *Cahiers du cinéma* magazine before becoming filmmakers, theorizing about film before putting their ideas into action. But other definitions of the New Wave include further groups: critics Michael Witt and Michael Temple also named the older 'Left Bank' (and left wing) filmmakers Agnès Varda and Alain Resnais, and 'satellite' figures including Jacques Demy and Jacques Rozier. Cinéma vérité documentary makers such as Jean Rouch are sometimes also included, as are more commercial filmmakers that include Roger Vadim and Louis Malle. Characteristically, none of these filmmakers necessarily agree on any definition of the New Wave, nor who was included in it, unlike the Surrealists or the New Hollywood, who had at least a vague idea of community.

> In 1959, we were living a dream – everything was happening in ways that would have been inconceivable two years earlier.
> François Truffaut, 1988

That said, there are certain features to the era. Many of these filmmakers were strikingly young – Truffaut and Godard made their first films in their 20s, *The 400 Blows* (1959) and *Breathless* (1960) respectively – and they almost universally rejected the conventional apprenticeship route into French filmmaking, instead offering one another financial and moral support to get their first short and feature films made. This gave them remarkable artistic freedom, even if they were limited by shoestring budgets. The young Turks in particular shared writing and editing duties, cast friends in acting roles, and borrowed family apartments, cameras or vehicles. They relied on inheritances and loans to buy film stock. They would even give one another film credits to help build their reputations and establish 'experience' in the industry to secure financing for the next person's film, while each filmmaker who achieved success would reinvest money in the next project ready to go. These budget limitations meant that they shot on public streets with ambient sound and natural lighting, helped by newly developed lighter cameras, often in only one take, and without established stars or expensive studios.

In search of imperfection

More importantly, their choices rejected the French 'tradition of quality' that had previously dominated the national cinema, with theatrical language, lavish production values and established stars. Their position, as discussed in the 'auteur' theory essay, rejected such work as mere craftsmanship rather than artistry; the New Wave films would be personally driven, diverse and based in cinema rather than theatre. The budget limitations inevitably gave them a

Angry Young Men movement

The French New Wave was paralleled in the United Kingdom by a not entirely dissimilar movement in theatre and film called the Angry Young Men. The term, coined to promote John Osborne's play *Look Back in Anger* (1956), came to refer to a mostly working-class group of playwrights and filmmakers who used the spontaneous, sometimes near-documentary, style of the French New Wave to bring British working-class life to the screen. Notable figures included Tony Richardson, Karel Reisz and Lindsay Anderson, with breakout films including *Saturday Night and Sunday Morning* (1960), *The Loneliness of the Long-Distance Runner* (1962) and *This Sporting Life* (1963). The movement proved less lasting than the French, however, as more obviously commercial British hits took off in the United States (*Tom Jones*; 1963 and *A Hard Day's Night*; 1964) and these 'kitchen sink' dramas were confined to the sidelines.

feeling of realism and spontaneity, without what Truffaut called the 'icy perfection' of previous French films. But they sought truth as a virtue in itself, not only out of necessity because they could not afford artificiality.

The Cannes Film Festival 1959 proved a sort of coming-out party for the movement, with Alain Resnais' *Hiroshima Mon Amour*, François Truffaut's *The 400 Blows* and Marcel Camus' *Black Orpheus* winning acclaim and prizes (Truffaut had been banned from Cannes just a few years before, after writing the essay that kick-started the auteur theory). However, while audiences largely embraced these daring new films, it was not all smooth sailing. The film journal *Positif*, as late as 1962, described the movement as 'an unruffled display of contradictions, combined with shilly-shallying, hollow catchphrases, patriotic jingles and a breezy use of cliches' or, as an editor's note put it more briefly, 'very vague and not all that new'. However, the furious passion about cinema that these filmmakers possessed, and their self-determination to try new and daring things, was important in itself. Perhaps what is most important and interesting about the New Wave is less what it was and more the rules it rejected: it challenged would-be filmmakers all over the world to try new things, to experiment with new ways, and not to worry so much about what internet discussion would call the 'gatekeepers' who tried to stop them in their tracks and ask about their credentials. For these filmmakers, the ideas, and the expression of those ideas, was far more important than any formal qualification could be.

The condensed idea
A new, looser, more documentary style of filmmaking

30 Japanese golden age

Sometimes, a single decade can transform a country's national cinema. The roughly 10-year period from 1950 saw Japanese filmmakers produce a stream of widely acknowledged masterpieces, establishing Japanese cinema as a major presence on the world stage. Directors such as Akira Kurosawa, Yasujirō Ozu, Ishirō Honda and Kenji Mizoguchi made a lasting impact, helping to reestablish Japanese cinema after the war years, but also to permanently broaden its scope and ambition.

Japanese cinema history

Early cinema in Japan hewed closely to the traditions of its theatre, to the point that the Pure Film Movement grew among critics to encourage more cinematic techniques, a move away from Kabuki theatre and the development of a true local cinema. The country had a

Yasujirō Ozu

Yasujirō Ozu started his film career in the silent era, but would end up working with both sound and colour. Like Japanese cinema itself, he was initially influenced by Hollywood to the point that his films were said to 'reek like butter', a perjorative term for Westernized content. However, Ozu developed his own style and was later hailed for helping to cement a thoroughly Japanese cinema, using low angles, static shots on objects for scene transitions and very little camera movement. He also largely rejected the over-the-shoulder shot for conversation scenes, preferring to have actors look to camera as if the viewer is involved in the conversation, and frequently skipped the sort of big events that other filmmakers might focus on. But the result was understated masterpieces like *Late Spring* (1949), *Tokyo Story* (1953) and *An Autumn Afternoon* (1962).

thriving silent cinema industry well into the 1930s, since the cost of converting to sound delayed its adoption, but in the years prior to World War II the government's Film Law sparked a growth in film censorship and propaganda film.

> If I could have said it in words, I would have; then I wouldn't have needed to make the picture.
>
> Akira Kurosawa, quoted in *Akira Kurosawa Interviews*, 2008

Unsurprisingly the war years led to a significant drop in production, but also a more precipitous drop in foreign film imports, so that the local stories that did get made could flourish. This allowed filmmakers to develop Japanese cinema without American and other influences. By 1945, however, they had other concerns. Japan was a defeated nation, occupied by the Americans and under the Supreme Commander of the Allied Powers (SCAP), General MacArthur. These occupying forces also censored film, this time for any subjects considered overly militaristic, jingoistic, xenophobic, vengeful, anti-democratic, sexist or racist, pro-suicide or pro-feudal. This initially made it difficult to tell classic samurai stories, for example, and films about the war sometimes endured multiple re-writes.

The SCAP regime faded, however, even before the US formally left in 1952, and while some of its strictures lingered, allowing filmmakers to challenge some traditional ideas, the result was a sense of new possibility and opening up. Fresh talent, such as Akira Kurosawa and Toshiro Mifune, found their chance to make an impact, while older filmmakers like Ozu embarked on a new lease of creative life.

The golden years

The following years saw a creative explosion that was matched by the appetite of local audiences: viewership for Japanese films hit 1.127 billion visits in 1958. The end of the censorship regime allowed filmmakers to begin to process the war years and the devastation of the atom bombs, which they did in films as diverse as *Children of Hiroshima* (1952) and *Godzilla* (1954). Masaki Kobayashi focused on the war with *The Human Condition* trilogy (1959–61), while Mikio Naruse (*Floating Clouds*; 1955) communicated a new sense of indecision and melancholy.

Akira Kurosawa began the decade by winning the Golden Lion at Venice in 1951 and the Best Foreign Language Oscar for *Rashomon*, and followed that with an extraordinary run that included *Ikiru* (1952), *The Seven Samurai* (1954), *Throne of Blood* (1957) and *The Hidden Fortress* (1958). Director Ishirō Honda and special effects genius (and later director) Eiji Tsuburaya brought *Godzilla* to the screen, launching the modern *kaiju* (or giant monster) movie and challenging the United States on its home turf of blockbuster spectacle. *Gate of Hell* from Teinosuke Kinugasa in 1953 became the first Japanese film to win the Palme d'Or in Cannes, while Hiroshi Inagaki won an Honorary Oscar in 1955 for the first part of his *Samurai Trilogy*, before winning the Golden Lion at Venice for *Rickshaw Man* in 1958. Kenji Mizoguchi seemed to specialize in stories about women, winning acclaim for his run *The Life of Oharu* (1952), *Ugetsu* (1953) and *Sansho the Bailiff* (1954).

This era boasted films with huge spectacle and lavish design, but also closely observed domestic dramas that, in some cases, sought to draw attention to certain inequalities in Japanese society (Mizoguchi's portrayal of women; Imai Tadashi's *Darkness at Noon* from 1956) or to describe a new order (*Tokyo Story*). The string of Japanese contenders at big international film festivals established a virtuous circle: international distributors started paying more attention to Japanese cinema, resulting in more money flowing in to make more films. At least, in the short term.

The Japanese New Wave, decline and rebirth

A decline began in the mid-1960s, as the appeal of TV began to cut into the cinema market and reduce local box office, but it gathered pace after 1970. Even filmmakers like Kurosawa could not find local funding for their work, as film studios went out of business and independent producers tried to fill the gap. By the 1980s things began to tick upwards again, with Studio Ghibli establishing itself, anime taking off internationally, yakuza films finding local success and filmmakers such as Takeshi Kitano gaining fame at film festivals, but the sheer time it took to recover demonstrates the severity of the fall from those 1950s golden days. Some of the world's best filmmakers now come from Japan – Ghibli's Hayao Miyazaki, Hirokazu Kore-eda, Ryusuke Hamaguchi, Takashi Miike and Takashi Yamazaki, to name but a few – but the peculiar fervour of those years has never quite been replicated.

Toho Studios

Toho was founded as a general entertainment company in the 1930s, but came to play a huge role in the 1950s golden age. It was not only home to many of Akira Kurosawa's films, but was also responsible for launching *Godzilla* in 1954, its longest-running franchise and the character for which it is best known worldwide. It reasserted that legacy in recent years with the acclaimed *Godzilla Minus One* (2023), which the company self-distributed and helped to an Academy Award win for Best VFX. While many in the West know it chiefly as the home of that *kaiju*, it is responsible for the majority of Japanese box-office champions and is the country's largest film importer.

The condensed idea
A post-WWII explosion of Japanese film talent onscreen

31 Martial arts movies

There is a lot more to Chinese cinema than martial arts movies, but that vast industry has made a unique contribution to action cinema through these films. Audiences derive great pleasure in seeing people do things well onscreen, whether that is singing, dancing or spin-kicking someone in the head, and in the latter category the cinema of Hong Kong, Taiwan and mainland China has been preeminent. Others have imitated the form – think of Thailand's *Ong-Bak* (2003) or Indonesia's *The Raid* (2011) – but its native cinema is still its natural home.

Cinema origins

Chinese cinema dates back to 1896, when film demonstrations were held in port cities such as Shanghai and Hong Kong before spreading inland. Initially film production and national cinema centred around Shanghai, with technicians trained by Americans and the first local stars such as Zhou Xuan and Zhao Dan emerging. However, that began to change even before the bombing of Shanghai by Japan in 1932 (which destroyed many silent film reels) and its subsequent capture in 1937. Displaced filmmakers spread across China and began an era of less centralized production that reflected the country's diversity. Politics would shape much of Chinese film production thereafter, with the nationalistic propaganda of the war years replaced eventually by a Communist cinema that had to hew close to Party values. The Cultural Revolution led to a clampdown on film content and expression while, conversely, vastly growing the cinema audience, since the revolutionary government valued the power of film to communicate ideas. While Chinese cinema began to open up in the 1980s, filmmakers could still find themselves in hot water for work that was considered too nostalgic for an imperial past, or otherwise problematic. That, for a long time, limited the scope for historical epics, in particular.

> Martial art is a form of expression, an expression from your inner self to your hands and legs.
>
> Donnie Yen

The first martial arts films were part of an attempt to draw on specifically Chinese culture and history for storytelling inspiration. They provoked a political response. *The Burning of the Red Lotus Temple* (1928–31) by Zhang Shichuan is now lost, but is believed to have been the first martial arts film – or rather, serial (it was 27 hours long and ran in 16 parts). Its craze was such that the Chinese Nationalist Party then in power banned all *wuxia* films (see below) lest they provoke anarchy. That may be why the first breakthroughs in kung-fu cinema came from British-ruled Hong Kong.

When everybody was kung-fu watching

A craze for kung-fu movies began in the late 1960s and early 1970s, and was one that Hong Kong producers the Shaw Brothers and Golden Harvest studios were keen to meet. Early stars included Jimmy Wang Yu (*The One-Armed Swordsman*; 1967) and Cheng Pei-pei (1966's *Come Drink With Me*), but it was Bruce Lee who took the phenomenon global with his astonishing charisma and dazzling martial arts' skills in films such as *Enter The Dragon* (1973). A slump followed Lee's untimely death, but a new type of hero, the *xiaozi*,

The Shaw Brothers

The martial arts cinema of the 1960s and 1970s – and beyond – was shaped by the productions of the Hong Kong-based Shaw Brothers. Founded in 1925, the three Shaw brothers (Runje, Runme and Runde) built on a background in theatre, and then film distribution, to make Chinese language films, and in the early 1960s they helped to launch the kung-fu film, which began as a stripped-back response to the cliched and unconvincing fantasy of the *wuxia* films of the day. The brothers popularized the form along with Golden Harvest studios (founded by former Shaw filmmakers) and even co-produced Western films such as *Blade Runner* (1982).

would follow. This more mischievous and rascally figure would be more vulnerable and less composed than the unstoppable Lee model, but could still engage in spectacular displays of physical prowess. Alexander Fu Sheng was an early proponent, but the form was really perfected by Jackie Chan, whose combination of slapstick and skill has made him a global star across six decades. Even at times when kung-fu fell out of fashion around the world – and even in China, where there was some question over martial arts cinema tropes in the 1980s – Chan's comedy skills kept his work in the public eye, helped by his 'Three Brothers' collaborators Sammo Hung and Yuen Biao.

Since the 1980s stars including Donnie Yen and Jet Li have kept more dramatic martial arts films alive. Following more closely in Bruce Lee's footsteps, Li, in franchises such as *Once Upon a Time in China* (1991), built his career on particular grace and an impressive fluidity of movement, while Yen, who had to wait until 2008 to get his own franchise, *Ip Man*, is one of the finest all-around martial artists alive. Both have been part of a sort of outreach effort to Hollywood and other national cinemas: Li made *Lethal Weapon 4* (1998) and *The Expendables* (2010); Yen appears in *Star Wars: Rogue One* (2016). This demonstrates both their global star appeal (to filmmakers as well as audiences) and encourages global audiences to seek out their native cinema and the majority of their best work.

Wuxia

The release of Ang Lee's *Crouching Tiger, Hidden Dragon* in 2000 marked a new era of popularity for China's *wuxia* films (a Chinese historical/fantasy genre that covers chivalry and conflict in ancient Chinese history, sometimes with a supernatural element). These often also feature martial arts' elements, but are far less beholden to the laws of physics, glorying in wire work and other enhancements to achieve spectacular leaps and blows. *Crouching Tiger* was a huge hit and was followed by Zhang Yimou's *Hero* (2002) and *House of Flying Daggers* (2004) to similar acclaim. These films gave better roles to women than they had had since the 1960s, finding work for Cheng Pei-pei again, showcasing work by Michelle Yeoh and Zhang Ziyi, and bringing in stars like Maggie Cheung for good measure. But they also marked a new era for Chinese filmmaking, allowing the portrayal of a colourfully realized past without political backlash. With one of the biggest cinema box offices on Earth, a growing national film industry and increasingly diverse output, especially in the low-budget independent sector, the martial arts film may grow in surprising new directions.

The condensed idea
Action innovation in the kung-fu movie and *wuxia*

32 Indian film

India produces more films than Hollywood most years and boasts some of the most passionate film audiences in the world. A huge native population, widely spread diaspora and large fandom in countries such as China means that the Indian film industries play to an enormous number of people globally, making $1.9bn worldwide in 2022, for example. This is due to not just one, but several local industries that reflect the country's diversity and its lively culture.

For many people in the West, and for many decades, Indian cinema was synonymous with Bollywood, the colourful musical films from Mumbai (formerly Bombay, hence the 'B' in 'Bollywood') in Hindi or Urdu. This reflected a certain preference within India as well: independent films and those from minority language groups were not always given the same opportunities in distribution or funding as their Hindi counterparts. However, in recent years Telugu cinema – based in Hyderabad and boasting, in Ramoji Film City, the largest studio complex in the world – has challenged the (predominantly) Hindi cinema most associated with Mumbai at the Indian box office. Tamil cinema, Malayalam and Kannada also represent a significant slice of the pie.

History of Indian film

Indian cinema dates back to the 1890s, initially featuring the same semi-documentary films as other countries: boxing matches and nature documentaries. By the early 1910s, local talent such as Dadasaheb Phalke and Raghupathi Venkaiah Naidu emerged and began to build careers and industries in Mumbai and Chennai respectively. More than 1,000 cinemas were built across India, but more significantly there were seasonal and 'tent' cinemas that travelled the country, bringing fresh films to remote audiences. The first local sound film arrived in 1931, *Alam Ara*, a Hindustani fantasy, and quickly other national language groups started making their own talkies. Separate film industries grew up around the country, in cities such as Mumbai, Hyderabad, Chennai, Bangalore and Kolkata, among others.

After independence in 1947, Indian cinema enjoyed a golden age. Cinema had an influx of capital from wartime black-marketeers eager to invest their gains, but more importantly was seen as a means of cultural revival and expression to celebrate the new era of freedom from British rule (and British film censorship). The 1946 Cannes Palme d'Or winner *Neecha Nagar* from director Chetan Anand was an early socio-realist success, though it was not released in India at the time. The naturalist 'parallel cinema' of Satyajit Ray and Mrinal Sen was developed, to global acclaim, with cinematographer Subrata Mitra's work on Ray's *The Apu Trilogy* (1955–59) proving influential, and Mehboob Khan's epic *Mother India* (1957) becoming the first Indian film to be nominated as Best Foreign Language film at the Oscars.

Masala films

By the 1970s, just as stagnation threatened popular Indian cinema, the screenwriting duo of Salim–Javed, made up of Salim Khan and Javed Akhtar, emerged. They made gritty crime dramas that dared to discuss India's wealth gap (and which incidentally made the name of future superstar Amitabh Bachchan with efforts such as 1975's *Deewaar*). The duo also worked with director Nasir Hussain on a new genre called the 'masala' film: just as masala is a blend of spices, this

Satyajit Ray

Born in 1921 in Kolkata, Ray trained as a visual artist but loved film. The French filmmaker Jean Renoir encouraged his ideas, before a later viewing of Vittorio De Sica's *Bicycle Thieves* (1948) made Ray determined to become a filmmaker. His first film was 1955's *Pather Panchali*, largely funded from his own savings and shot over more than two years. That was the first film in *The Apu Trilogy*, chronicling the struggles of a high-caste boy to survive extreme poverty, the loss of his parents and eventually his wife. Following that work Ray made several films remarkable for their sensitive portrayal of women, and worked on everything from documentary to science-fiction work.

combines elements of melodrama or drama, action, comedy and romance, typically with song and dance numbers as well. *Yaadon Ki Baaraat* (1973) is generally considered the first of these, but with hits like 1975's *Sholay* these soon came to dominate and define the Bollywood film.

Bright colours and spectacular sets characterize these films, along with lengthy running times, the better to squeeze in all those story elements and tones. Given that the plots and characterization in many of these films follows quite standard forms, expert choreographers, song writers and action directors are sometimes more powerful in Indian cinema than in the West, and directors and producers can be a little weaker. That said, stars of Indian cinema are closer to the stars of classic Hollywood in status, fame and money-making potential than the A-listers of modern Hollywood, and they have considerable power to get films made: 2001's acclaimed *Lagaan* went into production because superstar Salman Khan took it on.

While the masala style is particularly associated with Bollywood, it proved popular across India. Salim-Javed held onto the rights to their

The Khans

Salman Khan, Aamir Khan and Shah Rukh Khan are not related, but have collectively dominated Bollywood films for three decades, after emerging in the late 1980s. Their nicknames – respectively, the Tiger of Bollywood, Mr Perfectionist and King Khan – give you some idea of their appeal. Salman has a near flawless run of hits, starring in the highest-grossing Bollywood film of the year a record nine times. Aamir has a lower output than the other two, but is considered to have very high standards when he does. 'SRK' is arguably the world's biggest movie star, with a massive following globally. Incidentally, 1950s megastar Dilip Kumar's real name was Muhammad Yusuf Khan, so he is sometimes referred to as the First Khan.

own films for South India, allowing remakes of Hindi hits in other languages. Some Indian films are filmed as 'multi-linguals' from the outset, shot in two or more languages to create near-identical localized versions of the same movie. In modern times, S S Rajamouli's *Baahubali: The Beginning* (2015) popularized the 'pan-Indian' film, shot in multiple languages and released concurrently nationwide. This helps to cut down on the sort of unauthorized remakes that plagued the early sound films, when language barriers first became an issue.

International acclaim and influence

The Bollywood style has proved popular with filmmakers worldwide, with Baz Luhrmann crediting it as an influence for his *Moulin Rouge!* (2001) and Danny Boyle tapping into it for 2008's crime drama/quiz show musical *Slumdog Millionaire*. Parallel filmmakers also have a huge legacy: Ray has been cited as an influence on François Truffaut, Martin Scorsese and James Ivory, who worked with Mitra later in his career. Finally, there are wider signs that Indian film is now accepted as mainstream in the West: 2022's hugely popular action fantasy *RRR*, from director Rajamouli and the Telugu cinema, won the first Oscar for an Indian film, taking home Best Song for *Naatu Naatu*.

The condensed idea
A lively and vibrant cinema culture – one of the world's most prolific and most popular

33 Third Cinema

This appears, on its face, to be a loaded term. However, it usually refers to the radical cinema of the 1960s that emerged in Latin America, Africa and a few parts of Asia. The British theorist Paul Willemen even argued that the term 'Third Cinema' could be applied to radical minority filmmakers from developed, or industrialized, countries, but that has been largely rejected by the filmmakers themselves. 'Third,' therefore, does not refer to the 'third world' and is not synonymous with that controversial term, but aimed to channel the radical and revolutionary spirit of the time onto the screen, and to challenge Western cinema's colonialist and capitalist attitudes.

Argentinian filmmakers Fernando Solanas and Octavio Getino (*The Hour of the Furnaces*; 1968) defined Third Cinema in opposition to, first, classic Hollywood and its imitators and, second, European arthouse and its offshoots, which included the Cinema Novo in Brazil. They argued that even the latter was constrained by the market in what it could do stylistically, and the subjects it could tackle, and that their new and more radical 'Third' cinema could go further and become 'the revolutionary opening towards a cinema outside and against the System'. This attitude was embraced around the world, falling into a general sense of revolution and upheaval at the end of the 1960s. It parallelled the rise of liberation theology, also centred on South America, which called for priority to be given to the needs of the poor in the Catholic church.

Definition and practice

Theorist Teshome Gabriel was one of the leading figures in defining the Third Cinema movement. In Gabriel's assessment, many of the relevant national cinemas had experienced a first phase of film history, where they attempted to emulate Hollywood styles, and a second phase, where they attempted to build a national cinema, often at the behest of nationalist or dictatorial regimes. Third Cinema is therefore also the third phase of this progression, where film becomes a tool for social and political change that could change or even upend the social order, as in Miguel Littín's *The Promised Land* (1972).

Third Cinema in this view is therefore 'managed, operated and run for and by the people', with everyday people's struggles and lives becoming the focus of filmmaking and their concerns taking precedence over government ideals. Admittedly, however, some Third Cinema was fostered by governments: both Cuba and Algeria supported radical, militant cinema after their respective revolutions, and there was a degree of state support for filmmakers in some West African countries. The former USSR also supported and trained some of these filmmakers in Moscow, including Ousmane Sembène (*Mandabi*; 1968) and Sarah Maldoror (*Sambizanga*; 1972). Argentina, however, was actively hostile to much of the philosophy behind the movement, so that filmmakers received no state support at all.

Third Cinema film was made possible by the new and lighter cameras that had become available, and increasingly sensitive film that allowed shooting outside studio conditions and on a small budget. This was no longer technology that required Hollywood budgets or a vast studio apparatus; it could be democratic. It was Solanas and Getino's philosophy that such films should be shot and even distributed outside the mainstream. They maintained that the French New Wave and Cinema Novo had both been stymied by that need to meet a commercial structure. A true anti-capitalist cinema, therefore, would engage in more intellectually focused distribution, with screenings followed by debates about the film, performance art or art exhibition, or at the very least, refreshments and discussion.

Limitations and decline

Third Cinema per se declined precisely because it never managed to supplant the capitalist system that its proponents identified as a problem, and because the international conditions in which it was born ceased to exist. By the mid-1970s, the revelations of Pol Pot's crimes in Cambodia and the excesses of the Cultural Revolution in China had shocked Leftist revolutionaries around the world, while the worldwide oil crisis and economic downturn prompted the politically inclined to look inward to their own countries. Worse, right-wing dictatorships rose to prominence in many Latin American and some African states, and proved markedly more hostile to radical cinema.

The ideals of the Third Cinema endure in the surviving political cinema of states and individuals across Africa and South America. The pan-African film festival FESPACO was founded in 1969, during the movement's heyday, to promote films primarily set on the continent and made by African filmmakers. While Solanas and Getina's roadshow model of screenings accompanied by debate and discussion has not supplanted the traditional cinemagoing experience, FESPACO, for example, has made a programme of screening locally made films to rural audiences, to show stories close to their own lives onscreen. The movement was not, therefore, in vain. Filmmakers such as Cuba's Tomás Gutiérrez Alea (*Memories of Underdevelopment*; 1968), Argentina's Raymundo Gleyzer (who made *The Traitors* in 1973 and was among those 'disappeared' by the country's dictatorship) and Solanas and Getina opened the door for a more flexible, DIY form of filmmaking that could be attempted by almost anyone. They also established that there is a value in people around the world telling their own stories on camera, and using the power of cinema to explain, depict or critique the world they see every day, laying the path for what Maori filmmaker Barry Barclay called 'Fourth Cinema', film by indigenous people about their own experience of life and colonialism.

> Third Cinema was in many ways an effort to extend the radical politics of the time into the realm of artistic and cultural production.
>
> Teshome Gabriel, *Third Cinema Updated*

The condensed idea
Disseminating radical ideas directly to peoples around the world

34 New Mexican cinema

Cinema in Mexico goes back a long way; the extensive and groundbreaking film coverage of the 1910 Mexican Revolution means it is arguably baked into the country's DNA. For decades of the 20th century, Mexico was enormously successful in distributing its films across Latin America and had supportive governments who fostered a local industry. But it also followed something of a boom-and-bust cycle and had long been in the doldrums when the emergence of a sudden rash of local talent raised its profile once again in the late 1990s. This movement was led by, and centred on, the 'three amigos': Guillermo del Toro, Alfonso Cuarón and Alejandro González Iñárritu.

> We came up in a very different panorama of what Mexican cinema meant to the country and to international audiences. We started changing some of the technical aspects, and the approach to genre. Now that is taken for granted.
>
> Guillermo del Toro, quoted in *Deadline*, 2023

It is worth noting what had gone before. The Golden Age of Mexican cinema ran from the mid-1930s to mid-1950s, when its production levels were among the highest in the world. There was considerable cross-pollination with Hollywood, with many filmmakers training across the border and bringing their new skills home. Mexican cinema of that era is sometimes criticized for being too derivative of Hollywood, as compared to some national cinemas further south, but it also dealt with recognizably Mexican subjects and themes. There was an attempt by the so-called Nuevo Cine group to revitalize Mexican cinema in the 1960s and 1970s, influenced by the French New Wave and by the neighbouring example of Cuba, but while these efforts opened up new themes and subject matter, they did not shake up the whole of Mexican filmmaking immediately. Production increased, but not originality.

Disaster and rebirth

Following a devastating fire in 1982 at the Cineteca Nacional, which killed five people and destroyed more than 6,000 Mexican films, there

Emmanuel Lubezki

A regular collaborator of Arau, Cuarón and Iñárritu, Emmanuel 'Chivo' Lubezki is the only person to win Best Cinematography at the Academy Awards on three consecutive occasions, for Cuarón's *Gravity* in 2013 and then Iñárritu's *Birdman* (2014) and *The Revenant* (2015). Known for his use of natural light and his love of long shots – sometimes with a Steadicam and sometimes with a 3-axis gimbal – Lubezki is one of the secrets to the three amigos' success. He helped to develop innovative filming techniques for the long, unbroken shots of *Children of Men*, and designed the groundbreaking lighting of *Gravity* with its VFX team at Framestore. Chivo is also a regular collaborator with Terrence Malick and has worked with Tim Burton, Mike Nichols and the Coen Brothers.

were calls for a rebirth. The Instituto Mexicano de Cinematografía (IMCINE) was established in 1983 to promote and grow Mexican film, and slowly began offering funding to more locally made films in the late 1980s and early 1990s. This came just in time for a new generation inspired by the American independent movement, as well as their own forebears. One early breakout hit was Alfonso Arau's *Like Water for Chocolate* in 1992, which landed a Golden Globe nomination for Best Foreign Language film, and Guillermo del Toro's *Cronos* followed in 1993 to considerable critical acclaim. Cuarón made his first film, *Sólo con tu pareja* in 1991 with support from IMCINE, which got him sufficient attention to go to Hollywood and build his career abroad with *A Little Princess* (1995) and *Great Expectations* (1998). Del Toro, too, had a sojourn in Hollywood working on *Mimic* (1997) and *Blade II* (2002) when production in Mexico seemed slow to start.

At the end of that decade both returned to Mexican filmmaking, and the new era really began. What is generally considered the starting bell is Iñárritu's *Amores Perros* in 2000, a multi-linear psychological drama. That was swiftly followed by *Y tu mamá también* in 2001, from Cuarón, about two male friends (Diego Luna and Gael García Bernal) posturing about sex in an attempt to, perhaps, ignore their own feelings for one another. Bernal also starred in 2002's *The Crime of Father Amaro* from director Carlos Carrera, about a priest who seduces a teenage girl. Del Toro, meanwhile, returned home with *The Devil's Backbone* in 2001, a ghost story set in a Spanish orphanage. It began to seem that there was something in the water, especially when the three amigos all made Oscar-nominated films in 2006: *Babel* from Iñárritu, *Pan's Labyrinth* from del Toro and *Children of Men* from Cuarón.

New horizons

The secret of their success may be simpler: the three met one another early in their careers and formed a mutually supportive ecosystem that remains to this day, offering sometimes extremely harsh criticism of one another's films to achieve the best results. Del Toro credits Iñárritu's (Oscar-winning) *Birdman or (The Unexpected Virtue of Ignorance)* (2014) for spurring him to make his (Oscar-winning) *The Shape of Water* in 2017. Iñárritu says that *Cronos* changed his conception of what was possible in Mexican cinema. Both the other

Amores Perros

Iñárritu's first film tells three stories, connected by a car crash. The dark, crime-ridden plot concerns disloyalty, violence and inequality, without much sense of a happy ending. Iñárritu was already friendly with Cuarón, who had given him comments on the script, and Cuarón brought in del Toro to look at Iñárritu's final edit, which he thought was still too long. Del Toro agreed and convinced him to cut it down, and the *'tres amigos'* were born. The film premiered at Cannes and was nominated for Best Foreign Language film at the Oscars, opening this new era.

two were blown away by Cuarón's *Children of Men*. However, other Mexican directors are considered part of the Nuevo Cinema movement, including the likes of the Mexican American Carlos López Estrada (*Blindspotting*; 2018), Alonso Ruizpalacios (*Museo*; 2018), Issa López (*Tigers Are Not Afraid*; 2017) and Jonás Cuarón (*Desierto*; 2015) Alfonso's son.

By the 2010s, Mexican cinema was in its healthiest state in decades, partly as a result of this run of hits. In 2017 a record 176 films were made in the country, and audiences had doubled since the mid-2000s. Cuarón and Iñárritu made intensely personal, Mexico-based films in recent years with *Roma* (2018) and *Bardo, False Chronicle of a Handful of Truths* (2022) respectively, while del Toro's most recent hit was a 2023 animated retelling of *Pinocchio* that also tackled the rise of fascism. The clear New Mexican Cinema influence on, for example, the French film *Emilia Pérez*, which won the Jury Prize and Best Actress prize at Cannes in 2024, suggests that the impact of these films goes far beyond the country's borders, and that Mexican cinema's wider sway has been expanded considerably.

The condensed idea
A new, reinvigorated Mexican cinema

35 Nigerian film

Covering some 300 languages beyond the dominant Igbo and Yoruba cultures, as well as some Ghanaian stars and a number of films that shoot in English, the Nigerian industry is one of the world's largest by volume of output, with some 2,000-plus films per year coming out of the thriving studios of Lagos, Abuja and Onitsuka.

Nigerian cinema is part of a much broader tradition of African cinema, which emerged against the odds in the post-colonial period. Colonial governments had made no effort to introduce filmmaking technology to countries on the continent, instead exploiting its locations and history to tell their own narratives of white supremacy and 'savage' locals. A typical colonial film barely featured African people; look at *Pepe Le Moko* (1936) or *The African Queen* (1951), where the adventures of white characters are in the foreground and the locals mere supporting players. Despite such structural injustice, North African cinema, especially in Egypt and Tunisia, managed to find its feet early on, but it took longer for countries further south. There was a serious lack of infrastructure not just in film production, but even in exhibition, with rundown cinemas, unreliable projectors and a lack of sound equipment by the 1970s and 1980s. The film often cited as the first, full Nigerian feature was actually directed by the American actor and activist Ossie Davis in 1970, *Kongi's Harvest*. Its crew was non-local but the production company was Nigerian, and future Nobel Prize winner Wole Soyinka both wrote the script (from his own play) and starred. However, silent film *Palaver* was made there in 1926, albeit with a British director and a wildly racist outlook, while the Latvian born Sam Zebba shot *Fincho* there with non-professional local actors in 1957.

There were steady attempts to develop a cinema industry in Nigeria during the 1970s, but it was the arrival of VHS that changed the game. The new format made it quicker and cheaper to make films, and vastly easier to distribute and watch those films around not just Nigeria, but its neighbouring states. At times of unrest and violence, and with memories of civil war and dictatorship still very much alive, it sometimes seemed safer to watch films at home than in a crowded, public place – not to mention the fact that areas of Sharia law in the

Is Nollywood OK?

This term, used to encompass the entire Nigerian film industry, is somewhat controversial. That is because it is not something that emerged from Nigeria itself to describe its film industry, but something attributed to it from outside. The term was first used by New York journalists at the turn of the millennium and is therefore treated with understandable suspicion by home scholars of Nigerian film, wary of neo-colonialism and of any attempts to glibly dismiss the industry. The term riffs on 'Hollywood' and perhaps also its derivative term 'Bollywood'. That said, the success of Nollywood Week in Paris in 2024, showcasing Nigerian film, shows that it is by no means universally considered offensive or inapt.

north of the country have, at times, barred women from cinemas. But the nature of VHS also made 'Nollywood' an industry based on speed. Rest on your laurels after completing one film for too long and pirates would begin to eat into your profits, or unauthorized remakes to appear – possibly in other languages. The first major blockbuster of this new system was Chris Obi Rapu's *Living In Bondage* in 1992, and it was followed by waves of films through the 1990s and 2000s especially trying to capture its strange appeal. Nigerian filmmakers moved with the times, so that the early years of films shot very cheaply on grainy DVD have now given away to much higher-resolution digital filmmaking and distribution, removing some of the visual disparities between 'Nollywood' and higher-budget film cultures.

Nollywood films tend to be heavy on similar themes of violence, dark magic, poisoning, robbery and suicide. Blame that on a history of political unrest and violence, perhaps, or a desire for cathartic release in the safety of the television screen. However, there are lots of other genres produced: *Osuofia in London*, for example, was a two-part comedy hit that outgrossed *The Lord of the Rings: The Return of the King* when they faced off on release day in Nairobi, in 2003. The

Hausa films of 'Kannywood' or Kano, in the north of the country, historically showed a much stronger Bollywood influence, with frequent musical numbers, until an ultra-religious regional government began to censor its more flamboyant moments.

It all makes for prolific but not always artistic results. The fact that most Nollywood films were designed to be shown on the small screen means that they were not historically shot for aesthetic impact or appeal but for emotional intensity. The average budget for a Nollywood film in 2024 was about US$60,000, and shoots took around 12 days on average, though some are significantly cheaper and a few cost much more. However, films like *Lionheart* (2018) and *Mami Wata* (2023) have achieved international recognition and show that Nigerian films can travel far and wide, and with filmmaking technology becoming steadily better and cheaper, Nigerian filmmakers are now using VFX, AI and animation alongside everyone else.

Living in Bondage

This 1992 hit from Chris Obi Rapu tells a highly dramatic story of a man struggling to get ahead in life and turning to ritual sacrifice to achieve his aims. Andy (Kenneth Okonkwo) agrees to sacrifice his beloved wife to a curse by a satanic cult to gain fame and fortune, but comes to regret his bargain. He eventually repents and finds peace worshiping with evangelical Christians. The film was released in two parts and sold 200,000 copies on VHS, making it a sort of *Birth of the Nation* or *Star Wars* moment for the Nollywood industry in terms of its huge return on investment and cultural impact. A sequel, *Living in Bondage: Breaking Free*, appeared in 2019, with a now-ordained Andy facing the cult of 'The Six' once again and attempting to take down billionaire evildoers. It became the 11th highest-grossing film of all time in its home country.

The condensed idea
Impactful stories on
ultra-low budgets

36 Dogme 95

Most major world film movements have arisen organically, with perhaps a shared aesthetic but little in the way of a common cause. Dogme is unusual because it came from a statement of principles, set out by two idealistic filmmakers, about the way they planned to work. Many of those principles were ultimately honoured more in the breach, but it still proved influential in reinvigorating the independent film scene in Europe from the mid-1990s, and uniting a group instinctively opposed to a more and more complex filmmaking landscape.

The movement was announced in March 1995, in Paris, at a conference celebrating the first century of filmmaking. Danish filmmakers Lars von Trier and Thomas Vinterberg handed out red pamphlets describing the principles of Dogme and establishing a 'manifesto' of the movement. The pair aimed to create a new, low-fi extreme in filmmaking, in response to the big-budget Hollywood style that the movement explicitly rejected. Two more Danish directors, Kristian Levring and Søren Kragh-Jacobsen, officially joined the movement that year. Later

> [Dogme] was revolutionary, and then overnight in '98 in Cannes, it became fashion. Dogme became a free ride to all festivals in the world and a recipe for success. When the risk is gone it's no longer revolt.
>
> Thomas Vinterberg, 2017

proponents include the American Harmony Korine, France's Jean-Marc Barr and Spain's Juan Pinzás. Von Trier and Vinterberg were building on von Trier's approach to his breakthrough film, 1996's *Breaking the Waves*, even though that did not, in the end, adhere to all the rules of the movement.

Dogme (Danish for dogma) was a strict set of rules that they called the 'vow of chastity'. These mandated shooting on location with no outside props, artificial lighting or non-diegetic sound. The camera must be handheld, shooting in colour, without filters or optical effects, and using Academy-ratio 35mm film. The film itself had to be set in the present day, without 'superficial action' (no murders or guns), and genre movies were not acceptable. Finally, the director should not be credited and should impose no personal style on the film. In that respect the movement represented a rebuke to auteurism, though it is worth noting that Dogme's initial manifesto mimicked some of the language of François Truffaut's original auteur essay.

The purpose of Dogme

The idea of all these strictures was that filmmakers would make a virtue of their limitations and focus entirely on performance and storytelling, rather than fiddling with lighting or effects. The idea was inherently anti-establishment, almost entirely rejecting the 'bourgeois' taste that demanded clean, well-lit images and carefully composed sets. Perhaps surprisingly, the movement was not generally confined to first-time filmmakers struggling to get their debut off the ground, but was more often adopted by established directors. Some saw a chance to stretch their filmmaking talents and challenge themselves. Some, perhaps, sought to hitch their cart to a successful and trendy movement; others saw a chance for greater creative freedom in the low-budget strictures of the 'vow of chastity'. Many of their films hung

No wave cinema

This was a predecessor of Dogme, but had a similarly punk approach. Developed in New York's Lower East Side in the late 1970s, 'no wave' was inspired by the musical movement of the same name and emphasized a guerilla approach to filmmaking. Like Dogme, it sometimes relied on shock value for impact, but it also used humour and improvisation and a gritty, edgy aesthetic to challenge the mainstream. Filmmakers including Jim Jarmusch, Lizzie Borden and Amos Poe were fuelled by the vibrant underground culture of the time, and used the abandoned buildings of downtown New York as their playground. The movement petered out by the mid-1980s, but its spirit lives on in American independent cinema and it captured a moment of cultural fervour.

It is a term almost universally rejected by the filmmakers to whom it applies, but 'mumblecore' describes a loose group of mostly American, semi-improvisational independent films made in the 2000s and 2010s. These were distinguished by naturalistic acting and dialogue, which tends to be more important than any traditional plot. Most concerned the personal lives of 20-somethings, and were shot digitally on a usually low budget. Filmmakers like Andrew Bujalski (*Funny Ha Ha*; 2002), Mark and Jay Duplass (*The Puffy Chair*; 2005), Joe Swanberg and Greta Gerwig (*Hannah Takes The Stairs*; 2007 and *Nights and Weekends*; 2008) and Lynn Shelton (*Humpday*; 2009) are sometimes described as mumblecore. Horror films with a similar aesthetic may be termed 'mumblegore'.

around 'social discomfort, even emotional brutality' in the BFI's words, but there were Dogme romantic comedies and farces as well as dramas and satires.

The first fully Dogme-certified film (Dogme #1) was Vinterberg's *Festen*, followed swiftly by von Trier's *The Idiots*, both of which debuted at the Cannes Film Festival in 1998. The former, a family drama about historic abuse and lasting hypocrisy, won the Jury Prize and considerable acclaim; the latter, a tale of people simulating mental disability in order to behave outrageously, sparked a firestorm of controversy for its depiction of unsimulated penetrative sex (porn industry stand-ins were used, which was, appropriately enough, considered a breach of the Dogme vow of chastity). Many of the subsequent Dogme films would struggle to achieve the same prestigious start, but *Festen,* in particular, showed that the approach could work.

However, that was arguably never the point; nor, really, was adherence to the full vow of chastity. Dogme filmmakers could 'confess' to breaches of the rules and be forgiven: Søren Kragh-Jacobsen, for example, confessed to covering a window with a black cloth while making *Mifune's Last Song* in 1999, thereby bringing in a prop and artificially interfering with lighting. He also chased chickens from a neighbour's plot in front of the camera and hung a photo in one scene 'not as part of the plot, but more as a selfish, spontaneous, pleasureable whim', according to his confession. There was a jokey, mocking feel to some of these confessions: Harmony Korine's confession on *Julien Donkey Boy* in 1999 included the revelation that he had asked star Chloe Sevigny to wear a fake pregnant belly, and an apology for failing to actually get her pregnant.

The women of Dogme

While the founders were an all-male group, the movement was notable for a relatively high percentage of female directors, with four Danish women getting a boost from their work in the movement. For example, Lone Scherfig made *Italian for Beginners* (Dogme #12) in 2000, and Susanne Bier followed with *Open Hearts* (Dogme #28) in 2002. Both won international acclaim and prizes at the Berlin and Toronto Film Festivals respectively. Since female directors have historically worked with lower budgets and less institutional support than their male colleagues, the appeal of the movement to women perhaps makes sense: one might as well make a virtue of necessity.

Only 35 films were ultimately 'certified' by Dogme, and Pinzás was the only filmmaker to have had more than one Dogme-certified film. Still, certified Dogme films came from both Americas and Asia as well as Europe; it was an international movement in the end. In 2005, the collective was officially disbanded, ostensibly because digital filmmaking had achieved many of the movement's aims in democratizing film production. However, its spirit persists in independent films such as Sean Baker's *Tangerine* (2015) and films that meet at least a few of its vows still emerge each year.

The condensed idea
Making an art of the basics

37 The auteur theory

This is the most important concept in film analysis, which makes it strange that it is also one of the most controversial. Essentially, auteurism is the idea that the director is the closest thing a film has to an 'author', and that his or her work should be analysed as a body in the same way that a playwright or poet's work might be assessed en masse.

This does not sound controversial today, perhaps, but it was by no means obvious in the early days of cinema. Initially cinema jobs were not particularly well delineated or defined, and anyone might do work that we would now considered to belong to a director, producer or screenwriter more or less interchangeably. This was a time when films had officially been deemed mere commercial products rather than an art form, by no less an authority than the Supreme Court of the United States (in *Mutual Film Corp vs Industrial Commission of Ohio*, 1915) in a 9–0 decision that stood for nearly 40 years.

Andrew Sarris

The English term 'auteur theory' was created by critic Andrew Sarris, who also popularized the term in the English-speaking world in the 1960s. First in essay, and then in book form, he analysed film from the point of view of what its director added to the mix. His 'tests' of auteurism were three part: Is the director technically competent? Does the body of work show personality? And does the work betray interior meaning? If the answer to all three was affirmative, the director could be considered an auteur. Critic Pauline Kael, who vociferously resisted the notion even while famously championing key New Hollywood directors, considered all these criteria self-fulfilling and decried the notion of tests because 'criticism is an art, not a science', but Sarris's framework helped to popularize the serious discussion of filmmakers' bodies of work.

That said, as early as 1916, director (and screenwriter, editor, producer, actor) Lois Weber was arguing in print that, 'A real director should be absolute. He (or she in this case) alone knows the effects he wants to produce, and he alone should have the authority in the arrangement, cutting, titling or anything else that may seem necessary to the finished product. . .We ought to realize that the work of a picture director, worthy of a name, is creative.' Weber was partly arguing for her own importance, of course, as a very highly paid and respected director at Universal Studios, but she considered herself an ambassador for the cinema industry as a whole. German film theorist Walter Julius Bloem followed her in the 1920s, also identifying the director as having the key artistic role, followed by work by American playwright and screenwriter James Agee, and French critic André Bazin.

One barrier in the industry's attempts to classify film as 'art' was that it was hard to identify a singular artist, which was deemed necessary by many scholars – never mind that endless anonymous early relics and even Europe's Gothic cathedrals had no named genius behind them. It took some time for a consensus to emerge among philosophically minded critics that this artist figure might be the film's director. A key moment was an essay by critic (and future filmmaker) François Truffaut in January 1954's *Cahiers du Cinéma* called 'A certain tendency in French cinema'. In a blistering polemic (he was only 22 at the time), he decried the tendency he identified in certain 'quality' films to simply put a script onscreen, ideally one hewing as closely as possible to a great work of literature, without much artistic interpretation of psychology or subtext. He called instead for a *cinéma d'auteur* that would recognize the great contributions made by gifted directors, noting in passing that he did not consider anything unfilmable (in, it is implied, the right hands).

This idea was built upon and developed by Truffaut and his contemporaries, and popularized in the English-speaking world by Andrew Sarris. Gradually, studio filmmakers such as John Ford, Howard Hawks and Alfred Hitchcock were reassessed in the light of this theory, as critics examined the ways in which they had stamped their work with their own preoccupations, ideas and style. Previously, studio-made product had almost universally been considered non-artistic, but the auteurist critics made it possible to reexamine even popular films for interior meaning. Jacques Tati and Jerry Lewis were also considered auteurs by these early critics, who respected comedy more than many American writers.

The theory does, however, have serious limitations. It inevitably gives primacy to the contributions of a director in what is, after all, a collective art. Great directors tend to gather great collaborators, and so auteurism risks denying full credit to, for example, towering editorial talents like Thelma Schoonmaker or Anne V Coates, or important cinematographers such as Jack Cardiff and Christopher Doyle. Producers can arguably have an auteurist streak – look at David O Selznick or, more recently, the fingerprints of Kevin Feige all over the Marvel Cinematic Universe. Screenwriters may also make an outsize contribution, as with Mae West (*She Done Him Wrong*; 1933), Charlie Kaufman (*Being John Malkovich*; 1999) or Aaron Sorkin (*The Social Network*; 2010). The primacy of auteurism can downplay all these other roles. It can also be used to justify monstrously bad behaviour on the part of some directors, who used their high status to essentially abuse performances out of actors:

Can women be auteurs?

'Auteur' has, historically, been a fatally gendered term. None of the original auteurist essays named a single female director – something that is perhaps inevitable given that, at the time they were written, many silent films had been lost or dismissed as early, misconceived experiments, so it would have been impossible to fully consider the body of Alice Guy or Lois Weber's work. Agnès Varda gradually fought her way onto some lists of auteurs, but few women were acknowledged as such alongside her until very recent times (think Coralie Fargeat, Marielle Heller and Greta Gerwig). In the same way that women are not, historically, readily described as geniuses, they were not accorded the status and respect that the title of 'auteur' might attract.

Otto Preminger trying to remake Jean Seberg in his own preferred image, for example, off-screen as well as on it.

That said, the theory has been useful for directors of brilliant, but less obviously commercial films, attaching an air of importance to their work that might draw investors even where their box-office receipts do not meet expectations. Paul Thomas Anderson has had very few major box-office hits, for example, but still commands high budgets quite often because he is considered an auteur, and studios want to (occasionally) be seen to make art. Film stars may take significant pay cuts to work with directors they admire: both Leonardo DiCaprio and Brad Pitt reportedly took pay cuts to make *Once Upon a Time in Hollywood* (2019), while Andrew Garfield worked for scale on Martin Scorsese's *Silence* (2016). Auteurism has been instrumental in establishing excellent filmmaking as a viable basis for a career, and in more widely establishing film as an art form.

The condensed idea
The director as 'author'

38 Marxist film theory

The explosive rise in popularity that film enjoyed around the world in the first years of the 20th century was extraordinary, but perhaps it should not be considered surprising. The general social and political turmoil of those times was equally febrile, with a wild sense of unrest that only grew during the upheaval and chaos of World War I. One of the strains of political and social thought that was most popular in the early years of the century, and that would dominate in Russia from 1917, was a Marxist worldview. It came to play a significant role in film history as well.

A way of looking at the world

Based on the ideas of 19th-century writers Karl Marx and Friedrich Engels, Marxism itself is a socio-economic analysis of society, looking at the material conditions of a society, the economic activity – farming and industry, say – that occurs in that society, and the ways in which that activity meets the needs of the people living there. Marxism theorizes that, in a capitalist society, conflict will arise between the minority who own the means of production and the majority who do the producing but do not share in the wealth that emerges. In contrast to the class struggle that must result in their view, Marxists may advocate for a socialist society where ownership would be cooperative and everyone's needs would be met. The individual must, therefore, take second place to the collective: to quote *Star Trek II: The Wrath of Khan* (1982) the needs of the many outweigh the needs of the one.

The Soviet Revolution of October 1917 in Russia attempted to impose a Marxist system, though arguably it never achieved a perfect one. However, it did attempt to impose a uniformly Marxist outlook in its art, including film. Soviet filmmakers were under considerable pressure to ensure that their approach to filmmaking and storytelling supported Soviet ideals. That meant less emphasis on the individual and more on groups; more consciousness of class struggle and an emphasis on the nobility of the worker over mere aesthetic appeal (Soviet filmmaker Sergei Eisenstein was accused of paying insufficient attention to this priority). Techniques such as the Soviet montage helped Eisenstein and others to keep the emphasis on group action, and to tell stories effectively without traditional narrative structure. The official cultural doctrine of the Soviet Union and its allies was eventually semi-codified as 'socialist realism' (not social realism), which was in fact heavily stylized and prescribed to uphold the ideals of the Soviet state and its government.

> We must look for the essence of cinema not in the shots, but in the relationships between the shots, just as in history we look not at individuals, but at the relationships between individuals, classes etc.
> Sergei Eisenstein, 1926

Historical forces always shaped where Marxist ideas were able to influence cinema. Arguably no mainstream American and very little Western European cinema was ever truly Marxist, but certainly the 1950s campaign by Senator Josephy McCarthy against 'Reds' in Hollywood ensured that the major US film studios would shy away from even mildly left-wing content for more than a decade for fear of being smeared as 'fellow travellers', until the counter-culture movement of the 1960s revived Marxist ideas and fired them with new life.

In the mid-century, certain terms of Hollywood's Production Code were even used to control political content. One aspect addressed the need to ensure that films would not cause any diplomatic incidents with friendly countries, which in practice often amounted in the 1930s to not insulting Hitler. Censorship was a tool used extensively against Marxist filmmakers. Right-wing regimes in South America supressed attempts to launch a leftist cinema there, whereas Castro's Cuba actively supported a thriving film industry. However, Marxist analysis still engages with hostile cinema traditions to examine exactly how and why a Marxist film would look different from the ones we see.

Marxist analysis

Marxist theory extends far beyond Soviet Russia. Broadly, it is a means of analysing both the form and content of a film in terms of the messages it sends about class, wealth and systemic inequality. Film, in this view, cannot be separated from the economic and social conditions in which it was made, or those in which it is seen. As with gaze and queer film theory, Marxist theory means approaching film with an awareness of facts beyond those presented onscreen, and holding an awareness of ideas that the film may not appear to consider important or relevant.

There have been some filmmakers whose work employed Marxist ideas or ideals without necessarily identifying with the term. French Marxist filmmaker the young Jean-Luc Godard (who later identified instead as a 'humanist') used parody to subvert the status quo and promote the class consciousness that Marxism deemed essential in *La Chinoise* (1967) and *Tout va bien* (1972). In the modern day, Oscar-winning filmmaker Bong Joon-ho has successfully portrayed class struggle and inequality onscreen in films that include *The Host* (2006), *Snowpiercer* (2013) and *Parasite* (2019), while Andrea Arnold (*Fish Tank*; 2009), Sean Baker (*The Florida Project*; 2017 and *Anora*; 2024) and Hirokazu Kore-eda (*Shoplifters*; 2018) have put class and economic hardship at the centre of their work. While strictly Marxist film theory therefore remains a fairly niche concern, many of the same ideals and priorities are widely discussed and praised – much like Marxism itself.

Ken Loach

He is generally described as a socialist rather than a Marxist, but Ken Loach is probably the most consistently outspoken and successful left-wing filmmaker on Earth. He has won more prizes at Cannes than almost any other filmmaker and has had more films debut in competition than anyone else, for work dealing with issues including homelessness (*Cathy Come Home*; 1966), social injustice (*I, Daniel Blake*; 2016) and the treatment of refugees (*The Old Oak*; 2023). 1969's *Kes*, probably his masterpiece, is a striking condemnation of the British educational establishment and a vivid depiction of poverty. If Marxist film has not taken over the world stage, Loach's 60-year career shows that an appetite exists for the honest depiction of social inequality.

Tendency films

Japan's 'tendency films' of the 1920s and 1930s are a good example of a consciously left-wing cinema attempting to spread its ideals through popular mainstream films. 1929's *A Living Puppet* and 1930's *What Made Her Do It?* were both hits, the latter becoming the highest-grossing film of Japan's silent era and reportedly causing riots with its depiction of an exploited girl turning against her oppressors. However, even as some leftist theorists rejected these films for their populism and lack of political rigour, the right-wing government of the 1930s clamped down on them. Some of the directors responsible were sent for re-education in prison camps, while others denounced their previous work and instead made films reaffirming the status quo.

The condensed idea
The examination of cinema through a Marxist lens, possibly towards Marxist ends

39 The gaze theory

In the mid-20th century, an overwhelming majority of filmmakers were male, and theories about filmmakers tended to be male focused without necessarily being aware of that fact. That began to change with the 'second wave' feminist movement of the 1970s, as a generation of women's rights activists fought for equal rights in the workplace, and in film criticism. This new cadre of film theorists brought a new way of thinking about film.

The first suggestions that something was changing in how film was discussed came from two critics, Marjorie Rosen and Molly Haskell. These two wrote books in 1973 and 1974 respectively, examining women's place in Hollywood history and finding it wanting. They found women primarily confined to long-suffering girlfriend and wife roles, or portrayed as femmes fatales and objects of desire without much internal life. They noted the significant over-representation of sex workers in cinema, and comparative lack of serious examination

What is the female gaze?

You might conclude that the female gaze would simply be the opposite of the male gaze: Chris Hemsworth with his shirt off instead of Halle Berry, say. However, Mulvey's view was that the female gaze is more rooted in curiosity than simply another type of objectification – a view of possibility and exploration. The term is more often used to refer to films made by female directors and/ or cinematographers. Some characteristics are female leads who may be stunning but are not overtly sexualized, who meet with men on a basis of mutual or growing respect and equality.

of motherhood, sisterhood or female friendships. Both took issue with the tendency among the crop of then-emergent New Hollywood directors to continue to prioritize male protagonists over female, and macho subjects over feminine ones. Rosen argued in *Popcorn Venus* that film shaped society 'because of the magnetism of movies – because their glamour and intensity and "entertainment" are so distracting and seemingly innocuous – women accept their morality and values. Sometimes too often. Too blindly. And tragically.' Haskell, in the blistering *From Reverence to Rape: The Treatment of Women in the Movies*, found that onscreen, 'Far more than men, women are the vessels of men's and women's fantasies and barometers of changing fashion'. She analysed how men's stories were prioritized over women's, and how Hollywood perpetuated the 'big lie' of our society: that men are superior to women.

Visual pleasure and narrative cinema

An argument that was slower to build steam, but longer lasting, came from Laura Mulvey, who as a film-obsessive student in 1973 wrote an essay titled 'Visual Pleasure and Narrative Cinema'. Mulvey argued, among other things, that classic Hollywood cinema assumed a male viewer. Its films therefore catered to the perceived desires and priorities of that viewer, who was also assumed to be cis, heterosexual and probably white. The very form of cinema focused on bits of female bodies, not the whole person. Male characters onscreen might therefore be point-of-view characters because that would be easy for this assumed viewer to identify with, while women tended to be portrayed as objects of desire, or mere adjuncts to a male story. Mulvey theorized that, for many women to enjoy a film, they had to adopt what she termed a 'metaphorical transvestism' and adopt the viewpoint of an almost certainly straight, cis, white, able-bodied male. That might not be a problem if it happened only some of the time, but the asymmetrical weight given to male characters meant it was hugely dominant.

It's extraordinary the way [the gaze theory] has persisted. It's rather like the monster at the end of the movie. Every time you think it's gone. . .

Laura Mulvey, 2021

This came to be known as the 'male gaze' theory of cinema. Mulvey was building on the concept of the gaze in art, discussed by art critic

John Berger a year earlier, which explained inter alia why there are so many more female nudes in the great art collections than male. These ideas also stemmed from Jean-Paul Sartre, who had discussed the philosophical concept of the gaze in *Being and Nothingness* in 1943. The act of looking, he said, created a power imbalance between the gazer and the subject of their gaze; the person being looked at is objectified, and it is the person looking who is the active party. The idea is also rooted in work by Sigmund Freud and Jacques Lacan, psychoanalytical theorists who discussed 'scopophilia', which is the desire to look at pleasant things, usually in a sexual or semi-sexual context. The cinematic experience, with beautiful people presented onscreen, satisfies this wish – but again, the question for Mulvey was whose wish precisely was being satisfied in this way, and her impression was that it was mostly that of straight, white men.

Developing an oppositional gaze

The Black intellectual bell hooks took this a step further, noting that the Hollywood films that informed Mulvey, Haskell and Rosen excluded Black people, and particularly Black women, almost entirely. In hooks's view, a Black female gaze must be 'oppositional': it must carry the awareness that one is excluded from the narrative and challenge not only the male objectification of women, but also the white supremacy that denies Black humanity. For hooks, 'There is power in looking. By courageously looking, we defiantly declared: "Not only will I stare. I want my look to change reality."' Absence is also a choice worthy of consideration and challenge: trans people and disabled people must make a similar assessment when they are unrepresented onscreen.

Similarly, many gaze theories have been criticized for their relatively simplistic understanding of the viewer. As well as gender there are questions of sexuality, gender identity, race, religion, class, and physical or mental disability that may shape a viewer's reaction to a film. Almost all these categories are poorly represented in mainstream film

A wider view of 'gaze' theory is simply one that encourages the film viewer to think about who made the film, who is the intended or imagined audience, and whose point of view, or imagined point of view, is therefore shaping what we see onscreen.

Laura Mulvey, filmmaker

As well as being a film theorist, and now a professor of media studies, Laura Mulvey spent much of the 1970s putting her views into action as an avant-garde filmmaker. Along with her husband, Peter Wollen, she co-wrote and co-directed six films including the influential *Riddles of the Sphinx* in 1977. Many of these investigated feminist ideas, like her writing, but also Freudian concepts and questions of theology. Mulvey saw avant-garde filmmaking as a challenge to the patriarchal traditions of the mainstream and a way to explore and change modes of representation, making it a continuation of her theoretical work.

The condensed idea
A way of deconstructing film by considering its relationship with its viewer

40 Queer theory

The long hangover of Hollywood's Hays Code, and similarly repressive social standards around the world, meant that there was, until relatively recently, very little representation of LGBTQ+ characters in mainstream film in many countries. Even arthouse and independent film tended to present gay and lesbian stories as tragedies, and the other letters barely at all. That began to change, slowly, in the 1960s and 1970s, helped along as a new generation of queer campaigners fought for recognition both of cinema's LGBTQ+ pioneers and also for all the ways that their stories were being excluded from popular culture.

The theory

As with the gaze film theory, queer film theory delves into both psychoanalysis and history to explore how LGBTQ+ people have been treated onscreen and behind the camera. But it goes further than that. Queer theory also challenges heteronormativity, the attitude that

Angers and Bowers

Two books, *Hollywood Babylon* (1959) by Kenneth Anger and *Full Service* by Scotty Bower (2012; with Lionel Friedberg) have purported to shed light on the many LGBTQ+ people living and working in classic Hollywood. Many of Anger's stories have been challenged or debunked, but Bowers was considered honest by those who knew him, and he spoke of the hidden gay or bisexual lives of many Golden Age stars. It is now clear that the repressive standards of the time led many stars to hide their sexuality and enter 'lavender' marriages to cover up their same-sex interests – think Rock Hudson marrying his agent's secretary.

assumes the primacy of heterosexuality in everyday life and in film characters, unless specifically asserted otherwise. Queer theory, and queer cinema, attempt to decouple the assumption of 'normality' from 'heterosexuality' only, and indeed the assumption of default cisgender heterosexuality where the question is not explicitly addressed.

For queer theorists such as Gloria Anzaldúa and Judith Butler human sexuality and gender identity do not divide simply between cis and trans, or straight and gay, as that would exclude non-binary or agender people and bisexual, asexual or pansexual people. This builds on the work of Sigmund Freud but also Alfred Kinsey in examining human sexuality and activity. Assumptions about sexuality and gender should therefore be interrogated more rigorously, as should depictions of gender and sex onscreen. Queer theory also looks at historical LGBTQ+ filmmakers to see what traces of that identity might have made it to their work, at a time when open discussion was impossible, or to see how modern filmmakers might treat queer issues.

The history

There were queer stories early in film history. There is a 1914 film called *A Florida Enchantment* where magic seeds turn women into men. The gay Swedish filmmaker Mauritz Stiller made *The Wings* in 1916, about a gay couple threatened by the designs of a conniving woman. *Different from the Others* (1919) was co-written by Marcus Hirschfield, a gay sex researcher. G W Pabst's *Pandora's Box* (1929) features a lesbian subplot, but then Weimar Germany was more open minded than the United States at the time. Such films were widely censored when they travelled.

For many years, the Hays Code prevented open depiction of LGBTQ+ characters in Hollywood, and where characters were implied or coded as such, they tended to be portrayed in a negative light: as perverts or buffoons. Vito Russo, whose 1981 book *The Celluloid Closet* was key in exploring how homosexuality had been treated in cinema, laid out the long history of film's suppression of gay identity. Russo assessed how LGBTQ+ characters had been treated in cinema. In his view, the 'big lie' of cinema as regards queer people was to deny their existence entirely; partly, but not only, because of the Production Code strictures on portrayals of LGBTQ+ life.

Classic Hollywood, therefore, was a closeted town. Queer stars were universally encouraged to hide their sexuality, and William Haines, who refused to enter a fake romance with a woman to hide his, lost his studio contract as a result. A few directors were able to function while being fractionally more open about their identity, though it was risky. George Cukor was able to manage a long career, but the premature end of James Whale's career in the 1940s suggests that homophobia may have been a factor. When gay people were present onscreen, they tended to be evil, tragic or merely tiny supporting roles in the lives of the straight leads of the film. The understanding of queer rights as a facet of civil rights grew significantly during the 1960s, even before the Stonewall riots of 1969, and the AIDS crisis of the 1980s further brought the unjust treatment of gay people into the spotlight. Both eras saw a small rise in sympathetic portraits of LGBTQ+ people.

> Hollywood is yesterday, forever catching up tomorrow with what's happening today.
> Vito Russo

Dorothy Arzner

It is not known today if Dorothy Arzner embraced the word 'lesbian' to define herself, but she dressed in daringly masculine clothes for her era, and spent her life living with another woman, choreographer Marion Morgan. She was also a rare female director in the Hollywood studio era, with a string of hits that featured major roles for female stars – like one of Katharine Hepburn's breakthroughs, *Christopher Strong* (1933) – and distinctly cynical views on conventional romance: see *Craig's Wife* (1936) and *Dance, Girl, Dance* (1940). Arzner retired from Hollywod in 1943, but would later teach film at UCLA to students including the young Francis Ford Coppola.

The New Queer Cinema

The New Queer Cinema or Queer New Wave of the 1990s was an independent film movement that included Jennie Livingston's *Paris is Burning* (1990), Derek Jarman's *Edward II* (1991), Gus Van Sant's *My Own Private Idaho* (1991) and Guinevere Turner and Rose Troche's *Go Fish* (1994). Cheryl Dunye's *The Watermelon Woman* (1996) is important for its depiction of Black women, and Todd Haynes's early films proved influential. With critical acclaim and inventive storytelling, these films helped to show that there was considerable appetite for queer narratives, and many queer directors got a start that helped them to bring diverse characters into Hollywood films.

In the modern-day mainstream, there have been efforts to tell more diverse stories and to include trans people for the first time and wider perspectives, but heteronormativity remains the norm for major releases. It is, however, now possible to have a successful directing career in Hollywood as an out-LGBTQ+ person, and many actors are now out of the closet as well, though there is a sense that some, even in recent times, have paid a career penalty for their openness. Films about LGBTQ+ characters, including *Philadelphia* (1993) and *Moonlight* (2016) have won major Oscars, though both were made by straight filmmakers.

Many studios blame this lack of diverse representation on the need to sell their films in countries with restrictive censorship regimes, but the result is often a paucity of stories in which those who identify as queer can see themselves reflected onscreen.

The condensed idea
Rejecting a cis, heteronormative lens to examine film from a wider perspective

41 Structuralist and linguistic film theory

The French film theorist Christian Metz said that, 'A film is difficult to explain because it is easy to understand', but these two film theories attempt to deconstruct and explain how film achieves that understanding. A depiction of a thing, place or person in film is much closer to the thing itself than a painting or literary description could be, but films still depend on a degree of understanding from the audience that goes far beyond the simple images onscreen. As such, film is a sort of language, with its own internal structure.

The theory

As the name suggests, linguistics is the study of the nature of language, which attempts to construct a general theoretical framework to explain what language is and how it works. Structuralism, sometimes called semiology, is a sub-theory of that philosophy that sees language as a self-regulating and contained system, defined by other elements in the same system. It grew out of the work of the Swiss philosopher Ferdinand de Saussure, who distinguished between language as an abstract concept (*langue*) and the words used to communicate in daily life (*parole*). He also suggested a difference between a 'signified' (*signifié*) and signifier (*signifiant*) – roughly, the meaning of a word and the word itself. So, there is the thing, the abstract idea of the thing, and a third means of communication that links the two. Collectively, the *signifié* and *signifiant* make a 'sign', and each sign gains meaning in relationship to, or in contrast with, other signs. In other words, we understand things in relation to other things.

These were very live ideas in the late 19th and early 20th centuries and were developed well into the 1940s alongside existentialism and psychoanalysis, both of which (among other things) sought to interpret the individual's relationship to, and experience of, the world, and to apply scientific analysis to the humanities. Even very early in cinema history, these ideas were considered in relation to cinema. The Russian formalists who began writing on literature in the 1910s also influenced Russian cinema. They attempted to define a science of criticism and analyse text methodically. They eventually fell foul of Joseph Stalin and Leon Trotsky because it was obvious even to tyrants that their strictly formal analysis of word use and form was not properly rounded in considering the full impact of art.

Structuralism in cinema

Translated into film, structuralism means that film transmits meaning to the viewer through images, sounds, codes and conventions that work similarly to spoken or written language. So, a shot of a clock turning quickly, or calendar pages flipping up and away, or newspaper headlines coming and going, is generally understood by audiences as film shorthand for time passing. A music cue may signal a character's arrival, or communicate a certain emotional state. Such innate understanding is not universal – studies in the 1920s by anthropologist William Hudson showed that remote peoples not previously exposed to pictorial art could not instinctively distinguish depth or three dimensions in a two-dimensional image – but does appear to be communicated quickly to children and people exposed to film for the first time.

This understanding is how we derive meaning from the series of sounds and images that comprise a film, so a film can be analysed in terms of what underlying themes or ideas it is attempting to communicate, and how well it succeeds in doing so. In structuralist terms a film critic or student is almost translating a film, like a text in a foreign language. Structuralism ties into, and was promoted alongside, the auteur theory, because the search for meaning and communication in film is a corollary of the presence of a single artistic vision behind the camera. It is also linked to psychoanalysis in attempting to assess and discuss what meaning an audience might take from a film, and to both modernism and postmodernism because it creates a framework for understanding of both text and metatextuality.

> The great thing about literature is that you can imagine; the great thing about film is that you can't.
> James Monaco, on film structure

Post-structuralism

As with all philosophical concepts, structuralism has its critics. These post-structuralists argue that the definitions of these 'signs' are not necessarily either valid or fixed in time, and that the structuralists themselves are so involved in the structures they are describing that it is impossible to objectively assess them. These critiques owe a major debt to the work of Claude Lévi-Strauss, the anthropologist who

Structural films

It is useful to distinguish structuralism from the separate structural film movement of the 1960s United States and 1970s United Kingdom. This was an experimental, avant-garde cinema that tried to strip film to its most basic elements to reexamine its power and possibilities. Structural films include Michael Snow's *Wavelength* (1967) which is a 45-minute zoom shot around a single room, shifting through colour, negative and monochrome among other small changes. The British arm of the movement was centred on the London Film-Makers' Co-operative and also played with the material properties of film itself, as in Peter Gidal's *Bedroom* (1971), which also zooms and pans around a room. That grew out of a 1960s counter-culture scene that also included Sally Potter among its early figures.

rejected the idea of the past as a more primitive time, saying instead that it was simply a different one, so that a structural relationship between idea and object, or objects, cannot be assumed to be stable or steadily progressing.

Post-structuralism is most clearly influential in its temporal criticism: it is obviously true that the context of a film can change the meaning we take from it. Films that are considered obviously and near-universally offensive now, such as *Song of the South* (1946) or *Triumph of the Will* (1935), were not necessarily widely considered so at the time they were made. Even quite recent films such as *Wedding Crashers* (2005) or *Horrible Bosses* (2011) had sexual assault storylines that were played for laughs in a way that is already eyebrow raising. So, the temporal context of a film can change our understanding of its content. However, Roland Barthes' 'The Death of the Author' essay in 1967, which basically argued that the author is not the sole or final person to determine a work's meaning, is also extremely important in post-structuralism. It allows each individual to settle their own view on a film's meaning without reference to some final authority. That has opened up avenues in criticism and film debate that particularly resound in the modern social media age.

The condensed idea
Explaining how film communicates ideas and concepts

42 Postmodernism

There is no exact definition of postmodernism beyond the idea that it is a rejection of, or successor to, modernism. It is a term used in literature, architecture, decor and thinking. Italian philosopher Umberto Eco described it as 'a way of operating' rather than a specific set of rules or ideas. That all said, it is most often used in film discussion to refer to a specific approach, and it is useful to understand that in context.

Pre-postmodernism

Postmodernism was, as the name implies, a reaction to modernism. Modernism was the late-19th and early-20th century movement that rejected traditional thought and means of expression and searched for new approaches. It grew out of urbanization and the relatively fast-moving new technologies of the time, as well as the cultural and psychological shifts of World War I, the rise of secular thinking and of

Quentin Tarantino

The startling impact of *Pulp Fiction*, with its non-linear, hyperlinked narrative structure and daring reinvention of pulp-fiction tropes, saw Quentin Tarantino hailed as a major filmmaking talent. A film fan with a bone-deep knowledge of genre and cinema history – particularly the B-movies of the 1960s and onwards – Tarantino has enjoyed a filmmaking career that is thick with allusions to, and riffs on, existing film works, which he often subverts with an added dose of violence, excellent screenwriting (but bad language) and a willingness to push boundaries. He has toured kung-fu movies, war movies, Blaxploitation and historical epic, but to all he has brought a willingness to turned tired tropes into something new. His Academy Awards' success and status as a Cannes darling suggest that he has also succeeded in elevating his material into something closer to 'high' art in film terms than the 'low' art that inspired him – another postmodernist approach.

scientific approaches. The rise of psychological analysis and Freudianism was also a huge contributor to the movement. Existentialism, and a focus on the individual, demanded new and more individual art. The results could be experimental, introducing abstract expression and an emphasis on subjective experience, but also acknowledged art's debt to previous works, incorporating adaptation and collage into much modernist work. In art, this led to a move away from depictions of primarily classical and religious subjects, usually created in studios, to freer and more adaptable movements that included Impressionism, Expressionism, Cubism and Dadaism, sometimes painted outside. In literature, it saw the decline of the generally rather wordy 19th-century novel in favour of a more experimental and sometimes stream-of-consciousness approach.

In cinema's case, this led to developments such as Soviet montage and German Expressionism and much of the groundwork of cinema. Surrealism, usually seen as the most extreme form of modernism (though some might be described as postmodernist), also derives from these ideas.

A definition of postmodernism

Postmodernism, in turn, rejected the air of self-seriousness that its proponents saw in modernism, for an approach that is sometimes more playful or counterintuitive. It riffed on, and reinvented, previous art forms, transforming low art into high and high art, sometimes, into pulp fiction. Postmodernism also embraced irony, turning away from modernism's sincerity in favour of, sometimes, mere style without substance. However, movements such as Marxist and feminist film analysis are often folded into the postmodern approach – they became popular, after all, largely in the postmodern period – and neither are much known for their playfulness. There, the postmodernism comes simply from the fact that such approaches interrogate the old ideas and may require a sense of awareness of structural inequalities beyond those presented onscreen. This also applies to LGBTQ+ theory, disability rights advocacy and all race theory.

The general mass of art described as postmodernist is sometimes dismissed by critics as simply being depthless. If everything is a reference to everything else, and the issue is more style than substance,

Wes Craven's 1996 hit *Scream* revitalized the slasher film horror genre, which had become stale and predictable, with an injection of postmodern self-awareness. *Scream*'s characters had seen classic slasher movies, knew the 'rules' to surviving a horror film and were determined to follow them. They therefore shared the audience's awareness of genre tropes, so that Craven and screenwriter Kevin Williamson could use that knowledge against both characters and audience to deliver twists and surprises from a killer (or killers) who were *also* aware of how slasher films worked and could play against those 'rules'. This deliberate invocation of, and undermining of, genre tropes makes the film postmodern even before one of the killers eventually reveals a motive – fame and fortune – that plays into the idea that life is all a game and nothing truly matters.

then is the whole thing merely performative irony? However, the commentary intrinsic to even parody and pastiche can have meaning, so that postmodern works such as 1982's *Blade Runner* can be taught alongside the noir films to which it pays homage. For some filmmakers, a postmodern approach is a tool like any other: just Eco's 'way of operating'.

Postmodernism onscreen

A film is usually described as postmodernist more because of its style than its small-p political content. Postmodern films are often a homage to, or pastiche of, older work. They may be self-referential or meta in their approach, letting a clued-up audience know that the film is aware it is a film even if, as theorist Noel Carroll suggested, the wider, clueless audience should still be able to enjoy it as a film without that knowledge. These films might consciously play with the rules and tropes of genre, mashing together genres for effect or attempting a sort of 'pop art' approach of turning low art forms or genres into high art. They may also challenge our expectations to break down rules of time and place that we have been taught to expect.

It will be immediately obvious that certain films meet some, or all, of these criteria: Quentin Tarantino's *Pulp Fiction* (1994); Shane Black's *Kiss Kiss Bang Bang* (2005); Joanna Hogg's *The Souvenir Part I* (2019). Wes Anderson's films have been described as postmodernist in their hyper-theatricality and eerie composition. Spoof films such as Zucker, Abrahams and Zucker's *Airplane!* (1980) are postmodern parodies of one, or multiple, other films, consciously playing with, and occasionally breaking, genre rules, and breaking the fourth wall to address the audience directly – though they would rarely be described as high art. Comic characters, like the superhero *Deadpool* (2016), who addresses the audience directly are also postmodernist.

A period film that uses anachronistic modern music, such as Baz Luhrmann's *Moulin Rouge!* (2001) or Luca Guadagnino's *Queer* (2024), might do so to circumvent the usual temporal distance in a period film and help us to identify with the protagonists. Similarly, the temporal shenanigans enabled by modern VFX technology and prosthetics, allowing actors to play their younger or older selves and even to interact with themselves – especially versions of characters they have already played in other films, like the Avengers time-travelling through their own past in *Avengers: Endgame* (2019) – is a sort of postmodern approach.

The condensed idea
Playing on other films, art and ideas to create something new

43 The Western

The Western was the primary Hollywood genre for most of the 20th century and persists into the 21st century, despite repeated claims of its demise. Partly, that was down to geography: the wide-open plains and mountains of the West were within easy reach of the early film studios, and the Wild West was cheap and easy to reproduce onscreen because its towns were cheaply built to begin with. But it was also because this authentically native genre offered endless scope for action, adventure, romance and crime, alongside – eventually – considerable room for social commentary.

A genre close to Hollywood's heart

There are two clear reasons why the Western swiftly became a major film genre. The first, its geographical proximity to the film studios, has already been discussed. A few hardy and pioneering souls, such as Nell Shipman, went further into the wilderness, but for the most part it was studio backlots and cheaply thrown-together saloons. The second was temporal proximity. Many figures of the Old West, including Wyatt Earp, Buffalo Bill and Annie Oakley lived long enough to appear on film (Jesse James Jr. played his father onscreen). The process of building their own legends that had begun in the 1870s with a flood of cheap novels and serialized stories continued into the early film era and entered the cinematic grammar.

The genre began as a quintessentially American one, relating and mythologizing the building of the country with tales of bandits and crime, conflicts with hostile local tribes and the search for a good woman and a piece of land to call one's own. Certain expectations were quickly encoded into the genre: the clearly moral 'good' guy (often a sheriff), the thoroughly despicable bad guy (usually an outlaw), the love interest, and perhaps some comic relief. It was an overwhelmingly male-led genre, but also an overwhelmingly popular one. Thematically, stories addressed the imposition of order on the 'wilderness', and of a personal code of justice on an unjust situation. They trumpet the rugged frontier spirit and play up the civilized nature of the settlers, while usually ignoring completely the humanity of the people already living on the frontier.

John Ford

John Ford made his first film in 1917 and his last in 1970, with 130 or so in between. Born in Maine to Irish parents, he moved to Hollywood and became a giant of the nascent industry, winning six Oscars including four as Best Director. While not all of his best films were Westerns, several of those he did make marked milestones in the genre. They include *Stagecoach* (1939), the melancholy, dark *The Searchers* (1956) and the myth-busting *The Man Who Shot Liberty Valance* (1962). As one of Hollywood's most famous progressives, but also one of its biggest names, he was uniquely placed to move the Western's politics forward.

Glory days

Weirdly, the first known Western is a British film called *Kidnapping by Indians* made in 1899, but it soon caught on in the United States and was a major presence in the silent era. The early studio talkies, however, largely ignored it; partly because of the difficulties of capturing sound on location, but also because it came to be seen as a pulpy, low-budget genre. That changed in 1939, with five big Western hits including Marlene Dietrich in *Destry Rides Again* and John Ford's hugely important *Stagecoach* with then B-list actor John Wayne in the lead. That story, about a disparate group crossing dangerous territory in a shared coach, was the first major Western to exploit the stunning imagery of Monument Valley, and helped make it so popular that it would eventually become a cliche.

For the next 20 years, Westerns were reinstalled as Hollywood's most important genre, a status cemented after McCarthyism deterred studios from any subject matter that might be considered un-American. The genre spawned imitators around the world. Spanish and Italian filmmakers started to copy the form, and Hollywood studios funded cheaper shoots in both countries. Filmmakers such as Akira Kurosawa would draw inspiration from Westerns, there would

Something of a virtuous circle existed between the Western and Japanese cinema, particularly that of Akira Kurosawa. *The Seven Samurai* (1954) influenced 1960's Hollywood effort *The Magnificent Seven*, most famously, while *Yojimbo* (1961) drew from John Ford's lone heroes and in turn inspired Sergio Leone's *Dollars* trilogy from 1964. Kurosawa's *The Hidden Fortress* (1958) then inspired George Lucas's *Star Wars* (1977), which also drew from classic Western tropes with its desert planets and saloon fight.

be 'masala' Westerns made in India, 'ramen' Westerns in East Asia and even 'Red' Westerns in Soviet Russia.

Revisionism, death and rebirth

The counter-culture movement and a growing cynicism hit the traditional Western in the 1970s, but it was a raft of cheaply made, long-running Western TV shows that really sapped away the genre's appeal on the big screen. However, the 1970s also saw a significant uptick in revisionist and neo-Westerns that used the form to critique the United States. This was not an entirely new phenomenon – 1953's *Shane* was far more internal and psychological than most and Nicholas Ray's *Johnny Guitar* (1954) was formally very different and subversive in its gender roles – but following Sergio Leone's 'spaghetti' Westerns (so-called because they were shot in Europe and usually directed by Italians) the counter-culture Westerns made efforts to depict Native Americans in a more rounded manner, to reconsider female characters and to reexamine the heroism of settlers to the Old West.

This flexibility and openness to change meant that, while the Western has occasionally been declared dead in modern times and certainly during its doldrums in the 1980s, it has never entirely gone away. The start of the 1990s saw the one-two punch of the Oscar-winning *Dances With Wolves* (1990) from long-term Western cheerleader Kevin Costner and then Clint Eastwood, Leone's long-term collaborator and star, made *Unforgiven* in 1992. Along with *The Outlaw Josey Wales* in 1976, this makes Eastwood perhaps the single most important figure in the revisionist Western.

Almost every Western made post-1970 has some element of revisionism to it, from comic-book Westerns like James Mangold's *Logan* (2017) to Martin Scorsese's intense, elegaic *Killers of the Flower Moon* (2023). There have been Westerns from Korea (2008's *The Good, the Bad, the Weird*) and set in the American South (Quentin Tarantino's *Django Unchained*; 2012), and 'meat pie' Westerns from Australia (*The Proposition*; 2005). There are space Westerns (*Outland*; 1981 and *Guardians of the Galaxy*; 2014) and experimental or 'acid' Westerns like Jim Jarmusch's *Dead Man* (1995). The form's malleable ideas around civilization and harsh environments, individual struggle and ideals, and chases, gunplay and saloon fights, mean it is never likely to entirely die out.

> Western stories have always been built around violent behaviour, a frontier of violence in man.
>
> Clint Eastwood, quoted in *Cahiers du Cinéma*, 1992

The condensed idea
Inspired by the history of America's Old West

44 Horror

A t its simplest, the distinctive feature of horror is that it scares the viewer. But that can be accomplished alongside humour or romance. It might be done without gore or monsters and simply by a profound sense of unease, or of the uncanny, or of transgression. It can even be toned down enough for child audiences (Henry Selick's 2009 *Coraline*, for example). Often, horror provides a cathartic sense of relief from our everyday worries by pointing out that things could, after all, be much worse.

Horror goes back almost as far as cinema itself. Georges Méliès, inevitably, dabbled in tales of demons and monsters almost immediately (*A Terrible Night*; 1896 and *The Cursed Cave*; 1898), while Lois Weber prefigured the slasher movie with the home invasion thriller *Suspense* in 1913. But the first true, golden age of horror came in the 1920s and early 1930s. Expressionistic filmmaking, especially in Germany, was well suited to the horror genre because of its emphasis on mood and sensation, and F W Murnau's unauthorized 1922 *Dracula* adaptation, *Nosferatu*, in many ways set the template for what would follow: slow, creepy dread, looming shadows and horrific monster effects, with 'trick' cuts to make the impossible seem real. Universal Studios built on this with a series of Gothic literary adaptations starring Lon Chaney in the 1920s. It then had two monster hits (pun intended) in 1931: Tod Browning's *Dracula* and James Whale's *Frankenstein*. Both were influenced by the German Expressionist movement and showed that audiences could endure horror films even without much comic relief, something that had previously been in doubt. They also just about skirted the repressive censorship laws of the time while remaining scary.

The first golden age of horror

World War II temporarily quelled appetites for the genre, with only occasional exceptions such as 1942's *Cat People*. Stars such as Bela Lugosi (*Dracula*), Boris Karloff (*Frankenstein*) and Chaney continued to work in the genre; indeed, they were largely type-cast by it. They were succeeded in the 1950s by another generation of horror giants – Peter Cushing, Christopher Lee, Vincent Price – while Whale and

Browning were followed by filmmakers like Roger Corman, Mario Bava and Dario Argento. The long, slow collapse of the Production Code allowed horror filmmakers scope for sometimes extraordinary levels of gore, nudity and exploitation in relatively mainstream releases, and Hammer Studios in the United Kingdom made a business of offering up scantily clad women to leering monsters in the late 1960s. George A Romero more or less invented the zombie movie in 1968, effectively tapping into a Cold War fear of social breakdown and the end of civilization. More importantly, breakout horror hits such as William Friedkin's *The Exorcist* in 1973, a rare horror film to garner an Oscar nomination for Best Picture (it lost out to *The Sting*), began to give the genre more cultural cachet. By the end of that decade, John Carpenter's *Halloween* (1978) had popularized the slasher movie and Stanley Kubrick was working on his adaptation of *The Shining* (1980). That would, however, be a rare Kubrick film not to receive an Oscar nomination, evidence that the genre was still considered somewhat disreputable.

That sense would only grow in the 1980s, even as horror reached new heights of productivity and audience on VHS, which offered a quick and dirty release of low-budget films designed to shock and titillate its viewers. Horror is a genre that historically has a low barrier

J-horror and K-horror

In the late 1990s, a new style of horror emerged in Japan, J-horror, which would prove hugely influential around the world, led by Hideo Nakata's 1998 *Ring*, his follow-up *Dark Water* (2002) and Takashi Shimizu's *Ju-On: The Grudge* (2002). These were notable for their sombre tone, unbearable creeping tension and building dread, culminating in the appearance of vengeful, violent ghosts. They were inspired by, but not beholden to, Japanese mythology and *yōkai* stories, and would prove enormously influential around the world. A South Korean version, K-horror, emerged a little later, and was more famed for its moral horrors around revenge, particularly Park Chan-wook's *Vengeance* trilogy.

Many Hollywood films are remade, but no other genre engages in remakes as often as horror. It has given us such classics as John Carpenter's *The Thing* (a loose remake of 1951's *The Thing From Another World*) and disappointments that include 2005's *The Fog*, based on Carpenter's 1980 film of the same name. The early 2000s saw a raft of horror remakes and prequels that far outnumbered any studio-produced original horrors that decade. All attempted to cash in on brand recognition of the (mostly) 1970s and 1980s originals while avoiding the steadily diminishing returns of the sequels that had slowly eroded the loyalty of their fanbases (1993's *Jason Goes to Hell: The Final Friday*, for example). This has continued through to the 2020s, with David Gordon Green's *Halloween* trilogy and new adaptations for Stephen King novels such as *It* and *Salem's Lot*.

to entry. Future A-list filmmakers such as Sam Raimi (*The Evil Dead*; 1981), James Cameron (*Piranha II: The Spawning*; 1982) and Peter Jackson (*Bad Taste*; 1987) made their name with horrors and stepped up to bigger budgets. But others were content to stay there, making whatever they wanted with little studio interference and for an enthusiastic audience. Dubbed 'video nasties' in the United Kingdom, a wave of low-budget, high-gore films flooded the VHS market, and thrilled a generation of horror fans. Big-screen horror seemed tame by comparison, though filmmakers David Cronenberg (*The Fly*; 1986) and Wes Craven (*A Nightmare on Elm Street*; 1984 and *Scream*; 1996) kept things bloody. Horror won its first Oscar for 1991's *The Silence of the Lambs* from Jonathan Demme, though that lies on the border where the genre meets thrillers and has not seen a general softening of the Academy's position on scary films.

Gorno vs elevated horror

In the early 2000s VHS-levels of shock would colonize cinemas, with the much more extreme torture porn of *Saw* (2004) or *Hostel* (2005), low-budget films that were marketed on their gore, made by filmmakers raised on the 1980s VHS era and doing a lot with small budgets. By contrast, the 2010s and 2020s have been more notable for a slightly genteel correction towards the thoughtfully conceived and beautifully shot trend of 'elevated horror', an obnoxious phrase that describes a very effective blend of still gnarly terror with complex psychological or social commentary in films like David Robert Mitchell's *It Follows* (2014), Jennifer Kent's *The Babadook* (2014) or Ari Aster's *Hereditary* (2018). But there have also been much more classic horror hits, with mini studios such as Blumhouse building themselves around classic horror subgenres like the haunted house (the *Insidious* films), demonic possession (*The Conjuring*; 2013) or scary dolls (*M3gan*; 2022).

The genre's sub-categories are legion, from the religious horror of *Rosemary's Baby* (1968) and *The Omen* (1976) to the folk horror of *The Wicker Man* (1973) to a rom-zom-com (romantic zombie comedy) like *Shaun of the Dead* (2004). Some horrors scare you with the 'body horror' prospect of your own flesh turning against you (Coralie Fargeat's *The Substance*; 2024), others with the end of the world (*A Quiet Place*; 2018 and *28 Days Later*; 2002). 'Found footage' horror has enjoyed some popularity, with characters filming their own demise against unforeseen forces (*The Blair Witch Project*; 1999 and *Paranormal Activity*; 2007). It is a vast pool. The only thing all these films must have in common to meet the definition is that they must be scary or unsettling; must make us question our own comforts and must leave real life looking a little better in comparison to what we have just seen.

> To me, the central thesis of horror in film and literature is that the world is a more frightening place than is generally assumed.
>
> Kim Newman, author, filmmaker and critic, *Nightmare Movies*, 2010

The condensed idea
Anything, as long as it is scary

45 Film noir

Film noir may be hard-boiled, but it is also hard to boil down. Literally, the term means 'black film', referring to both the darkness of its usually crime-related plots and the chiaroscuro lighting that defines its look. The term was developed retroactively, applied in the 1950s by French critics to a group of American films. Filmmaker and critic Paul Schrader attempted to sum it up in 1972, as a Hollywood film movement occurring between 1941 and 1958, influenced by American pulp fiction and German émigré directors. The definition is a good starting point, but the noir movement was not exclusive to film (it also spanned comic books, radio dramas and even 'crime jazz'), and if you dismiss later noir films as 'neo-noir', this

Billy Wilder

Polish-born and German-trained in film, Billy Wilder fled the Nazis in the 1930s and became a Hollywood stalwart for nearly 50 years. His 1945 crime drama *Double Indemnity* was one of the founding films of the noir movement, with femme fatale Phyllis Dietrichson (Barbara Stanwyck) seducing an insurance salesman (Fred MacMurray) in order to persuade him to help her kill her husband for the titular payout. Wilder followed that with *The Lost Weekend* two years later, a noir-ish drama about alcoholism that won the Palme d'Or and the Academy Award for Best Picture. Wilder's career lasted into the 1970s, and would include dark satire (*Ace in the Hole*; 1951), comedy noir (*Sunset Boulevard*; 1950), courtroom drama (*Witness for the Prosecution*; 1957) and outright farce (*Some Like It Hot*; 1959), albeit with some noir stylings. One of the greatest directors and screenwriters of all time across multiple genres, Wilder had an innate cynicism that was uniquely suited to noir.

definition rules out earlier films that unquestionably have at least noir elements, and which influenced the early noir films proper – for example, Fritz Lang's *M* (1931) or Howard Hawks's *Scarface* (1932).

What is noir?

Some critics have argued that noir is less a genre and more a mood, or even a perspective on life. Certainly, it depends less on storytelling tropes and more on a feeling. Nevertheless, there are certain elements typical of the genre, if by no means necessary or sufficient for a film to qualify as a noir. Many noirs feature a private detective, always world-weary and often scarred by deep personal tragedy or shortcomings. Typically they take a case in a city environment, and may have a plot set in motion by, or leading to, a femme fatale, a woman whose attractiveness poses a physical or moral danger to the protagonist. That protagonist is as often an anti-hero as a hero, someone who lives with crime every day, rather than a Miss Marple type for whom it is an occasional shocking intrusion. There may be a mystery to uncover or unravel (hence noir's frequent recourse to flashbacks), a threat of violence and, ultimately, a revelation of corruption or violence by someone in a position of authority. Noir films tend more towards twists of cruel fate than other crime dramas. Even if the good – or least bad – guy 'wins' in a noir, he could be deeply scarred by the experience, or lose something valuable to him.

Noir has a very pessimistic worldview. Noir women are not particularly politically correct, that's why we don't see many of them; but they're a hell of a lot of fun to make movies about.
Brian De Palma, *Creative Screenwriting*, 2015

Those are a few story elements that recur throughout the genre, as do stars that include Humphrey Bogart, Robert Mitchum and Barbara Stanwyck. Another common element is narration, often by the protagonist. Many of these narrations show striking self-awareness, with characters harshly describing their own shortcomings and failings, but they also tend to reveal how lost the protagonist is as the usually complicated plot unfolds around them. It is only when it is too late, in many films, that they realize what is going on and how terrible it is (the neo-noir *Chinatown* (1974) has one famous revelation that shocks even Jack Nicholson's unflappable Jake).

The psychology and politics of noir

It is no coincidence that the golden age of noir occurred during, or just after, World War II, when a generation reckoned with the darkness of war and of Nazism. It was a push back against the happy endings that the Production Code preferred. Even the noirs that conformed to the Code by having criminals punished or killed at the end of the film left little hope that the world was fundamentally better as a result. There is an anti-authoritarian streak to many of these films, with their cynical heroes and more cynical villains. Many of the filmmakers responsible were known for liberal-leaning politics, though by the end of the classic noir era it is more a counter-communism paranoia that shapes the stories. Either way, there is a sense that the protagonist is on his (usually his) own against an uncaring world, left to fend for himself. Many of the classic noirs were based on books by Dashiell Hammett (*The Maltese Falcon*; 1941), James M Cain (*Double Indemnity*; 1944 and *The Postman Always Rings Twice*; 1946), Raymond Chandler (*The Big Sleep*; 1946) or Patricia Highsmith (*Strangers on a Train*; 1951).

The femme fatale

The role of women in noir has been much discussed by feminist critics. On one hand, these women are often defined by their sexuality, set in contrast to the good girl that represents all that is safe and domestic for the male protagonist. On the other, the femme fatale has agency and desires of her own, expressed through sometimes labyrinthine schemes to snare the protagonist. 'She kisses him so that he'll kill for her,' said one poster for *Double Indemnity* of Barbara Stanwyck's Phyllis Dietrichson, a relatively common bargain for the genre. Brigid O'Shaughnessy (Mary Astor) in *The Maltese Falcon* (1941) was a borderline sociopath, and almost got away with her schemes. There is a transgressiveness to such power, especially for the time, so that many critics have identified a crisis of masculinity as a key component of noir filmmaking.

The genre's heyday may only have lasted 17 years, as Schrader suggested, but its influence remains strong today. Noir elements crop up far outside any original confines of the term. Ridley Scott's sci-fi thriller *Blade Runner* (1982) has a strong noir feel, while there have been comedy noirs from the clearly parodic likes of *Dead Men Don't Wear Plaid* (1982) to the less obvious *Fargo* (1996). Christopher Nolan's *Memento* (2000) mixes noir with an amnesia element; his *Tenet* (2020) crosses it with time travel. Films such as Rian Johnson's *Brick* (2005) showed that noir could work in high school, while Jane Campion's *In the Cut* (2003) gave it a feminist twist, as did Steve McQueen's *Widows* (2018). If noir is a state of mind, then perhaps it is no surprise to find it so enduring.

The condensed idea
A world-weary twist on the crime drama

46 The musical

The musical draws on musical theatre traditions that existed well before Hollywood, from light opera to vaudeville to the spectacular productions of the Ziegfeld Follies. The arrival of sound, however, demanded the use of music to tell stories onscreen, so that a generation of dancers and singers found work on the soundstages of Hollywood as well as the stages of Broadway. It remains a popular genre despite many attempts to declare it dead.

Early steps

There had been attempts at musical films even before 1927's *The Jazz Singer* ushered in the sound era, with thousands of short films on the Vitaphone system from 1926 demonstrating how attractive the idea was. However, it was that film's wild popularity and the beginning of the sound era that catapulted it to the top of Hollywood's to-do list. *The Jazz Singer* only had a few musical (or indeed sound) scenes, but with theatres converting to sound and studios anxious to cash in, full-blown musicals were soon in production. In 1929, *The Broadway Melody* won Best Picture at the Academy Awards and *Gold Diggers of Broadway* proved the box-office champion, setting a record that would stand for ten years. Studios made more than 100 musicals in 1930, but quickly oversaturated the market so that just 14 followed in 1931. However, the arrival of director and choreographer Busby Berkeley's signature look in 1933, combining military drill precision with inventive use of camera angles and impossible stages that took full advantage of the cinematic form, revived the genre.

Gotta dance!

Stars such as Fred Astaire and Ginger Rogers were able to build careers as musical specialists in the 1930s, and *The Wizard of Oz* (1939) showcased the genre's potential. MGM therefore set up a unit under Arthur Freed in the 1940s to develop a new kind of musical, resulting in the likes of 1944's *Meet Me in St Louis* and 1952's unbeatable *Singin' in the Rain*. In many of the early film musicals, characters had broken into song and dance because they were stage performers, often literally as part of a performance. The new approach

In the 2010s and 2020s, film marketers became wary of the hostility of some potential audience members (mostly straight adult men) to musicals. The result was a series of musical films whose early trailers downplayed or entirely omitted their musical elements – *Wonka* (2023) and 2024's *Mean Girls*, *Wicked* and *Joker 2: Folie a Deux*, for example. Lady Gaga, who starred in *Joker 2*, claimed at its Venice Film Festival press conference that, 'I wouldn't necessarily say that this is actually a musical. The way that music is used is to give the characters a way to express what they need to say, because the scene and dialogue wasn't enough' – almost a dictionary definition of a musical. The ruse did not help that film, but it is unclear in other cases whether the marketing won over enough musical sceptics to compensate for the loss of musical fans who might have been tempted to buy tickets had they known the film's nature (maybe they are presumed to be savvier).

was that song and dance would essentially erupt directly from a person's soul onto the screen, expressing their inner desires or dilemmas without spoken dialogue. Song and dance numbers therefore drove the plot forward along with the dialogue in between.

Many big Broadway shows successfully travelled to the screen in the 1950s, including *Gentlemen Prefer Blondes* (1953) from Howard Hawks and Fred Zinnemann's 1955 *Oklahoma!* By the 1960s the genre contributed to some huge hits (*The Sound of Music*; 1965) but also some of the decade's most notorious flops. The genre was a distinctly minority interest through the 1970s and 1980s, despite breakout hits like *Grease* (1978) and *The Blues Brothers* (1980). Even the darlings of the New Hollywood ran into trouble when they attempted musicals, with flops greeting Peter Bogdanovich (*At Long Last Love*; 1975), Martin Scorsese (*New York, New York*; 1977) and Francis Ford Coppola (*One from the Heart*; 1981). Directors, in spite, or because of, the fact that musicals are notoriously difficult to make, seem drawn to the form, yet the genre spent the 1990s relatively defunct in Hollywood cinema. At the same time, it was re-established in animation, which had a fondness for songs all the way back to *Snow White and the Seven Dwarfs* in 1937.

Despite the naysayers, the musical never entirely went away. *Chicago* won Best Picture in 2003, and films like *O Brother, Where Art Thou?* (2000) and *Moulin Rouge!* (2001) showed a sense of vitality that belied predictions of its demise. There was a mini-trend for adaptations of Broadway musicals that had themselves been based on films (2005's *The Producers*, 2007's *Hairspray*) but by the late 2010s a resurgence had begun in screen musicals written directly for the screen, like *La La Land*, which won six Oscars in 2017, and *The Greatest Showman*, a slow-burning box-office sensation the following year.

> I try to write songs that are necessary. It seems to be important to keep the pace going, because I think an audience senses when songs are merely reiterating what you already know, or when they're ahead of you.
> Stephen Sondheim, *The New Yorker*

Musical worldwide

The Hollywood musical, with its storied history and soaring production values, remains the most famous exemplar of the form, but it is far from unique. Indian cinema, particularly, but not only in Bollywood, is known for its often lavish musical numbers and its style has fed back into Hollywood filmmaking through dance numbers in films such as *The 40-Year-Old Virgin* (2005) and *Slumdog Millionaire* (2008). Jacques Demy's 1964 *The Umbrellas of Cherbourg* remains influential on the genre, as does his 1967 *The Young Girls of Rochefort*, and Spanish cinema had a major musical tradition from the 1930s on.

Perhaps most surprisingly, there were serious attempts to make musicals under Stalin in the Soviet Union, despite considerable difficulty in combining the necessary sense of glamour and escapism with the proper glorification of labour and equality. One result was Grigori Aleksandrov's *Volga-Volga* (1938) reportedly Stalin's favourite film even though its protagonists dream of mere musical success and poke fun at the local authorities. The appeal of the musical really must be universal.

Alan Menken

Disney Animation had spent much of the 1980s in a critical and box-office slump, until Jeffrey Katzenberg took over the studio's reins and determined to get back to its glory days. Starting with *The Little Mermaid* in 1989, composer Alan Menken and lyricist Howard Ashman were brought in to craft original songs to accompany their animated stories, which they did to the tune of two Oscars. They worked together again on *Beauty and the Beast* in 1991 to Best Picture nominated effect, and had started work on *Aladdin* when Ashman died. Menken continued to work on animated films into the present day (2024's *Spellbound*), winning eight Oscars and launching a number of Broadway musical spin-offs. He helped to solidify an expectation of exuberant musical numbers in top-tier animated films.

The condensed idea
All-singing, all-dancing storytelling

47 The action movie

The action movie per se is a relatively recent invention, though it has roots in the earliest days of film. It overlaps with, but is distinct from, Westerns, thrillers, kung-fu movies, crime dramas and noir. It has become one of the most reliably popular film genres in Hollywood, and has been successfully exported to many other countries around the world after conquering US filmmaking within only a few years in the 1980s. Its heyday is, arguably, over, eclipsed by more spectacular spin-offs such as the superhero movie. However, the last five decades suggest that you never count an action hero out too soon; the genre has a way of surviving.

Action origins

The first glimmers of what would become the action movie go back a long way. If all you require is a lone hero battling numerous bad guys to (usually) achieve his end, most Westerns would qualify. Car chases, shoot outs and fisticuffs existed almost at the very beginning of

Diversity in action

There were attempts, even in the 1980s, to make action movies with female leads such as Cynthia Rothrock, Grace Jones and Michelle Yeoh. However, these tended to be lower-budget, less well-promoted efforts, except for Sigourney Weaver in *Aliens* (1986) and Linda Hamilton in *T2: Terminator 2* (1991), which became action franchises in their second outing and at James Cameron's direction. Black stars got a boost when Wesley Snipes and Will Smith built impressive action careers in the 1990s, but it would be the 2000s before female leads Angelina Jolie, Milla Jovovich and Charlize Theron built serious action resumes. 'Geri-action' movies with older leads such as Liam Neeson (*Taken*; 2008) eventually followed, culminating in *Thelma* (2024), an action movie starring a 94 year-old woman with age-appropriate challenges.

cinema. However, the action film as we now know it is more of a state of mind. The action, as film academic Harvey O'Brien argues in his book on the subject, is the point. The hero, or anti-hero, of the action movie expresses his will through the action itself, and the movement becomes the point, purpose and expression of his character through the film. This gives the action movie an enormous sense of propulsion and pace, when well done, and a simplicity of approach that makes it easy to transport around the world.

There are elements of the action movie in some thrillers of the late 1960s and early 1970s, most notably in the early films of the still extant James Bond franchise, which started with *Dr No* in 1962, and gritty thrillers such as Peter Yates' *Bullitt* (1968), or Don Siegel's *Dirty Harry* (1971) and its sequels. William Friedkin's *The French Connection* (1971) had a car chase worthy of any of the action films that followed, and there was a taste of the sort of masculine banter that would characterize these films in Burt Reynolds's 1970s hit *Smokey and the Bandit* (1977) and from Richard Roundtree in the Blaxploitation hit *Shaft* (1971). The kung-fu film craze that had gripped the United States in the 1960s and 1970s, especially around Bruce Lee in *Enter The Dragon* (1973) also played a role. Many of these films centred on anti-heroes or mavericks, men who let their fists do the talking. But the action movie itself would be a little different.

> I see movies as pure entertainment. I try to stay away from films with heavy messages. I want to sell tickets, not slogans.
>
> Arnold Schwarzenegger in *The Last Action Heroes*, Nick de Semlyen

First Blood

In the 1980s, the rather melancholy post-Vietnam films of the 1970s, like *Coming Home* and *The Deer Hunter* (both 1978) were replaced by a nationalistic backlash that celebrated a more self-confident superpower. The Reagan era trumpeted self-resilience and optimism, even dynamism, and that was reflected in its cinema. Nothing was more dynamic than an action hero, many of whom were literally self-made in the sense that they had sculpted their bodies to the peak of muscular possibility.

Sylvester Stallone's breakthrough film, *Rocky* (1976), had been a fairly traditional sports drama. His next mega-hit was *First Blood*

Keanu Reeves showed, in *Point Break* (1991), *Speed* (1994) and *The Matrix* (1999) that it was possible to be an action hero without the sort of hyper-masculinity of Stallone or Schwarzenegger. His *John Wick* franchise (2014–25), was at least as violent as *Commando* (1985) or *Rambo III* (1988), but has a sense of wounded grief that not even Willis ever quite reached in the genre's heyday. Wick's crusade against the forces that run his improbable, assassin-filled world (after they kill his dog) could be read as another one-man army, but it seems markedly less capitalistic and imperialist than what came before. Rather than propping up an empire, Wick seems determined to take it down.

(1982), a post-Vietnam story of a veteran being targeted by small town police while travelling across the United States, and exacting violent justice upon them. In the same year, Austrian-born bodybuilder and actor Arnold Schwarzenegger had his first hit in *Conan the Barbarian*, and it was clear that there was an appetite for larger-than-life heroes, one-man armies in fact, taking on a hostile world. Both would become franchises, Schwarzenegger in *Conan the Destroyer* in 1984 and Stallone with the explicitly Vietnam-repudiating *Rambo: First Blood Part II* in 1985. From then on, it was off to the races. Schwarzenegger had another huge hit playing a bad guy in James Cameron's 1984 sci-fi action hit *The Terminator*, and played two quintessential action leads in *Commando* (1985) and *Predator* (1987). Stallone's Rocky and Rambo franchises both grew more nationalistic and bombastic through the decade, while he also essayed the buddy cop sub-genre in 1989's *Tango & Cash*.

Other action stars

Stallone and Schwarzenegger were quickly joined by all-American star Chuck Norris, and soon after by Bruce Willis, Jean-Claude Van Damme and Steven Seagal. All but Willis were trained martial artists, but it was Willis who became the biggest star with the near-perfect *Die Hard* in 1988 and, inevitably, its sequels. While martial arts could be a factor in these films – Jackie Chan would make similar movies throughout the 1990s – it was not enough to make you an action star. Chow Yun-fat, not a martial artist, is unquestionably an action star thanks to films like John Woo's *Hard Boiled* (1992).

The action movie tied in perfectly with the high-concept trend of the 1980s, proving remarkably replicable over and over again. Cop heroes such as 1987's *Lethal Weapon*'s Riggs and Murtaugh had a sort of reason to keep encountering terrorists, thieves and gangsters, and commandos (or, more often, ex-commandos) like Rambo would simply be thrown back into the action, but more often the inciting situation would simply be written off as bad luck attending the hero. 'How can the same shit happen to the same guy twice?' asked Willis's John McClane in *Die Hard 2: Die Harder* (1990). More accurate to ask, how could it not?

The arrival of a muscle suit you could just strap on in Tim Burton's *Batman* in 1989 sent shivers through the genre, but the action movie would not be eclipsed by superheroes for another decade and a half. Even now, it persists in a slightly older and wearier form, still taking on the world one henchman at a time.

The condensed idea
The lone hero triumphs against impossible odds

48 Comedy

The easiest, and most obvious, definition of comedy is that it should make you laugh. Some of the time, that comes as an element or mode of entertainment in another genre – think of the comic scenes in Shakespeare's histories, or the moments of levity even in dramas such as *The Godfather* (1972) or *Gone with the Wind* (1939). However, for comedy films as a genre and for its sub-genres, laughter is the point and the purpose of the endeavour. This makes it a sometimes high-risk undertaking – a thriller that falls short may still have a compelling storyline or impressive action sequences, but a comedy without laughs is uniquely disappointing. Exceptions include absurdist films that qualify as comedy without technically provoking laughter, but as a rule, comedy that is not funny is a true failure.

Slapstick

Comedy goes back as far as film itself. One of the Lumière brothers' early films was *The Waterer Watered* (1895), about a gardener getting soaked by his own hose in a clever little bit of slapstick. That was the beginning of a trend that would be polished and perfected through

Laurel & Hardy

Stan Laurel and Oliver Hardy were independently established stars when producer Hal Roach paired them as a team in 1927 to phenomenal success. They made 107 films together, including 23 full-length features, for more than 20 years, and toured the world with a live show until 1955, transitioning seamlessly from silent film to talkies. They were a study in contrasts: one tall and slim, the other shorter and rounder; one shy and self-effacing, the other bombastic and bossy. While both felt trapped by their screen persona at times – a recurring problem for comedians – their collaboration set a template that would be imitated for decades afterwards.

the silent era. With clever wordplay impossible, the art of slapstick and wider physical comedy would be taken to astonishing heights.

Mack Sennett was one pioneer of film comedy. He established Keystone Studios in 1912 and showcased major future stars, including Fatty Arbuckle, Mabel Normand, Bing Crosby, Gloria Swanson, Harold Lloyd and, of course, Charlie Chaplin. His troupe shared tips and helped one another along – Normand tutored Chaplin on screen acting when he began, for example. Chaplin and Lloyd soon set up alone and became major stars, Chaplin to a degree arguably never matched since. His Little Tramp persona and gentle comedy style helped to sell absurd situations and wild flights of fancy (think of the machine in *City Lights*; 1931). Lloyd, and soon Buster Keaton, took elaborate stunt comedy to new heights, using clever camera trickery to appear to hang off buildings and elaborate rigs to collapse houses around them.

Farce and ferocity

The arrival of sound quickly saw studios recruit comedy stars and playwrights from the theatre and vaudeville, who generally transitioned to the screen with considerably more success than the dramatic actors dropped into silent movies a decade or so before. Wit, wordplay and timing were the essential qualities, as stage shows were more or less directly translated to the screen, and both farce and comedies of manners took flight. The Marx Brothers, who had honed their jokes for decades onstage, became major stars at Paramount, RKO and then MGM; Mae West, who could not only write one-liners but also generate scandalous publicity, was at one point the highest-paid star in the pictures. This was also a time when writing became important: Anita Loos script-doctored other people's work to add gags and Ben Hecht was much prized for his fast-paced wit (*Twentieth Century*; 1934 and *His Girl Friday*; 1940). The screwball comedies of the 1930s depended almost entirely on clever writing, as did wartime satires such as Chaplin's *The Great Dictator* (1940). In the United Kingdom, Ealing Studio comedies such as *Kind Hearts and Coronets* (1949) mined laughs from social norms and the class divide at a far lower budget level than the US equivalent.

Outside of the sharp but bitter one-liners of film noir, the post-war years and well into the 1960s were notable chiefly from battle-of-the-sexes comedies such as the Doris Day career-girl films, *Pillow Talk* (1959) and *Lover Come Back* (1961), and the gentle raunchiness of the UK's *Carry On* films (1958–92). Later in the 1960s, however, a new breed of satire grew in films such as Stanley Kubrick's *Dr Strangelove or: How I Learned to Stop Worrying and Love the Bomb* (1964) and Mike Nichols' *The Graduate* (1967), reflecting the tumult of the times and increasing hipness of audiences. In the 1970s, absurdism seemed to take over in the Monty Python films and in Mel Brooks' genre parodies *Blazing Saddles* and *Young Frankenstein* (both 1974), while the 1980s saw the full spoof develop thanks to Jim Abrahams and David and Jerry Zucker, after films like *Airplane!* (1980) and *Top Secret* (1984). It also saw the development of a new crossover form, the romantic comedy or romcom, covering films as diverse as *Annie Hall* (1977), *When Harry Met Sally* (1989) and *Pretty Woman* (1990). Crossover comedy also became ever more important; some of the best

Does funny travel?

In the silent era, US comedy stars became global superstars, with audiences around the world embracing figures such as Chaplin and Keaton. However, the talkies put up barriers to understanding – something that is funny to Germans may not be funny to Argentinians and vice versa. Even British comedy did not always work in America. Word play obviously does not always translate, nor do references to pop culture events and local celebrities. Gestures may even have different meanings. This has resulted in cuts made for local audiences and tastes around the world, but also in attempts at substitution. For example, animated films in the 2000s made a practice of bringing in minor local celebrities to redub roles originally given to American newsreaders or TV hosts. Some comedies travel surprisingly well – *Women on the Verge of a Nervous Breakdown* (1988) and other Pedro Almodovar's farces, some Indian films and the occasional breakout such as Germany's *Good Bye Lenin!* (2003) – but otherwise national cinemas are full of national comic hits that were virtually ignored abroad.

gags of the 1980s are in action films *Beverly Hills Cop* (1984) and *Lethal Weapon* (1987), and audiences came to expect wise cracking alongside their heroism.

Gross out

In a continuing attempt to raise the comedy bar, a previously niche form of gross-out, scatalogical or sexual humour went mainstream in the 1980s following hits like *Animal House* (1978) and *Porky's* (1981). It came back with a vengeance in the early 2000s with the hit *American Pie* franchise and its imitators. The gentler, more observational James L Brooks comedy-dramas of the 1980s, such as *Terms of Endearment* (1983) and *Broadcast News* (1987) also returned in the looser, free-wheeling Judd Apatow and Nancy Meyers efforts, while romcoms started trying to recruit male viewers with male-focused efforts like *I Love You Man* (2009). It is also worth mentioning the 21st century rise in cringe comedy – comedy where the sheer social embarrassment of watching the protagonist evokes laughter. Consider Sacha Baron Cohen's work *Borat* (2006) or the much lower-key lack of self-awareness in something like *Frances Ha* (2012). The late 2010s, however, saw a general migration of pure big-screen comedy to streaming services, even before the Covid-19 pandemic accelerated that trend. At the time of writing, most comedy on the big screen is therefore in a hybrid form – action comedy, horror comedy – while more traditional forms survive elsewhere.

> For me, comedy starts as a spew, a kind of explosion, and then you sculpt it from there, if at all. It comes out of a deeper, darker side. Maybe it comes from anger, because I'm outraged by cruel absurdities, the hypocrisy that exists everywhere, even within yourself, where it's hardest to see.
> Robin Williams, in the *Los Angeles Times*

The condensed idea
Films that should make you laugh

49 Propaganda films

The power of film, and its popularity, quickly made certain governments around the world take notice of it as a potentially effective means of broadcasting the messages they wanted to communicate and, perhaps, suppressing those that they did not. One result was suppressive censorship regimes, the other was the sponsorship of films that said exactly what governments wanted to hear. This could include morale-boosting works of fiction, encouraging local patriotism or anger against the enemy, or more practical, documentary-style information films educating people on the war effort or encouraging good health, hygiene or behaviour. These were all propaganda films, and they were a powerful tool.

The birth of persuasion

The Spanish-American War of 1898 began in April with the sinking of the USS *Maine* and ended with a treaty that finally ended Spain's American empire that December. But it also inspired the first propaganda films, with Vitagraph Studios quickly rustling up a short called *Tearing Down The Spanish Flag* (1898), which showed exactly that: a Spanish flag being lowered and replaced with an United States flag. This was shot in a studio but prompted huge applause from audiences fired up by William Randolph Hearst and Joseph Pulitzer's jingoistic press reports of the same period. *The Independence of Romania* in 1912 is considered the first full-length propaganda movie, made with the help of the Romanian army.

> The propagandist's purpose is to make one set of people forget that certain other sets of people are human.
>
> Aldous Huxley, *The Olive Tree*, 1936

World War I naturally saw propaganda become a more potent force, with newsreels shown widely in the combatant nations. Germany was particularly quick off the mark in banning foreign films, touring its own pro-German films and even setting up the American Correspondent Film Company to try to promote US neutrality. When the US did enter the war after 1917, however, films such as Charlie Chaplin's *The Bond* (1918) emerged, made expressly to raise funds for the fight. The October Revolution of 1917 that led to the Bolshevik regime in Russia also brought a near-immediate determination to use film to communicate the new government's message. Lenin assumed that the job would be less about persuasion than education of the masses, since they were largely illiterate and therefore immune to leafleting campaigns. Film was a vital part of this 'agitprop', the vigorous effort to spread Communist ideals and prop up the State.

Goebbels and World War II

The run-up to the next major world conflict would see cinema propaganda reach new heights. Partly inspired by the Communist example and partly based on its own populist ideals, Germany's Nazi Party were quick to engage with film and to try to use it to promote their ideas – leading, incidentally, to an exodus of Jewish and anti-Nazi talent to Hollywood. Joseph Goebbels was the party's chief propagandist, and he ensured that all filmmakers had to join a Reich Film Department so that he could control all film output. He also staged, along with filmmaker Leni Riefenstahl, the enormous rallies

Casablanca

It is one of the best films ever made, a romantic thriller about two star-crossed lovers who reunite in wartime Casablanca, starring Humphrey Bogart and Ingrid Bergman. But Casablanca is also a propaganda film, put into production just months after the attack on Pearl Harbor brought the United States into the war (the story itself is set in December 1941, the same month as the attack). It includes a stirring call to arms for the demoralized French and those under the collaborative Vichy regime, those in occupied Eastern Europe and most of all the United States to enter the fight wholeheartedly. Just as Bogart's Rick sacrifices his true love, Ilsa, for the greater good of the cause, so US audiences would be asked to give up their comforts to win the war.

that formed the backdrop for *The Triumph of the Will* (1935), which were designed to look impressive onscreen.

Once World War II began and the Allies entered the fray, they scrambled to enter the same battle for hearts and minds, and to inform the populace about their government's new priorities. There were some masterpieces among the mass churn of content that resulted: Charlie Chaplin's *The Great Dictator* (1940); Michael Curtiz's *Casablanca* (1942); Laurence Olivier's *Henry V* (1944); Powell and Pressburger's *A Canterbury Tale* (1944). Even animation was employed, with Disney creating family-friendly propaganda like *The Spirit of '43*, with Donald Duck encouraging people to pay their taxes.

Post-World War II

Propaganda filmmaking continued to be a major tool throughout the Cold War and beyond. The House Un-American Activities Committee under Joseph McCarthy scared Hollywood into line with its priorities during the 1940s and 1950s, with prosecutions of suspected Communists and those who refused to 'name names' of Communist sympathizers. That was largely off-screen, but the result was that American films would act as a tool of US foreign policy and project an

Leni Riefenstahl

Two of the most influential filmmakers in history, D W Griffith and Leni Riefenstahl, also made some of the most noxious films in history. Two of Riefenstahl's films for the Nazi regime, *The Triumph of the Will* in 1935 and *Olympiad* in 1938, helped to glorify Hitler personally and the regime generally, using careful composition, clever camera angles and deliberate staging to share the Nazi vision of an invincible thousand-year Reich. A former dancer and actor, Riefenstahl had been a rare woman to make a film under the old Weimar regime, but her association with the Nazis ended her career, and she spent the rest of her life fighting accusations of war crimes after using inmates at a detention camp as extras in her final film, *Tiefland* (1954).

anti-Communist, pro-capitalist stance around the world, with little criticism of US politics between the end of the war and the late 1960s. Similarly, dissent was carefully controlled and suppressed in the Communist world, while the rest of the globe saw both cinemas vie for their attention and sympathies.

In the modern age, filmmakers Michael Moore and Adam McKay have attempted to make major political points in films such as Moore's *Fahrenheit 9/11* (2004) and McKay's *The Big Short* (2015). Most such efforts have been exactly as successful as their ability to hide their political purpose. Around the world authoritarian governments continue to attempt to regulate what their citizens can see, while organizations such as – for example – the US military will loan its expensive equipment to Hollywood productions on occasion, but only on condition that they are portrayed in a largely positive light. A bigger concern are the fraudulent claims promoted in films such as *2000 Mules* (2021) and the possibilities inherent in 'deep fake' technology and AI filmmaking to create convincing, but false, film footage. George Orwell once said that, 'In general, propaganda cannot fight against the facts, though it can colour and distort them.' That may not be true for much longer.

The condensed idea
Films can serve political ends

50 Science fiction and fantasy

These two genres are often lumped together – a tradition followed here – but while they overlap, and sometimes share a fanbase, the two are very different beasts. Science fiction imagines the existence of a future technology, science or social change that allows us to explore our destiny as a species in the universe; fantasy imagines counter-scientific creatures, powers or worlds to explore more esoteric and metaphysical ideas. Both offer the opportunity for dazzling visuals, creative special effects and daring flights of imagination.

These speculative genres have a surprisingly long and storied history in film, even if they remained on the fringe for much of the first half of the 20th century. The oldest narrative film we know of, Alice Guy's 1896 *The Cabbage Fairy*, was a fantasy (given that it centred on a fairy), and around the same time, her more celebrated contemporary Georges Méliès would begin to specialize in fantasy, as in *The Astronomer's Dream* (1898) and science fiction, which included his Jules Verne adaptation *A Trip To The Moon* (1902). Fritz Lang's *Metropolis* in 1927 was a dazzling display of sci-fi imagination that continues to influence not only cinema, but also sci-fi literature and even music (Janelle Monae's debut album *The ArchAndroid*, for example).

However, after the end of the silent era both fantasy and sci-fi struggled. Occasional huge hits such as *King Kong* (1937) or *The Wizard of Oz* (1939) were the exception rather than the rule. The problem was that the demands of early sound were technical and prohibitively costly and adding the elaborate special and visual effects demanded by most sci-fi and fantasy films was simply too much trouble and expense. Both also suffered from a (continuing) perception that they are a little childish, though in the following decades work by filmmakers Stanley Kubrick and Andrei Tarkovsky would belie that characterization.

The state of the art improved gradually. The 1950s were boom years for science-fiction publishing, and some filmmakers inevitably tried to cash in on the trend, notably the prolific Roger Corman, who plied an eight-decade career in tightly budgeted B-movies, most of them in genre, and gave some titans of the industry their first jobs. With the dawn of the nuclear era and the start of the space race there were films about alien visitors (*The Day The Earth Stood Still*; 1951) and giant, mutant monsters (*Godzilla*, *Them!*; both 1954). More urgently, the 50s and 60s saw Hollywood desperate to compete with the rise of television, with basic dramas and small-scale Westerns struggling and US cinema began to seriously engage with the more spectacular prospects of imaginative genres to prove its relevance. Stanley Kubrick's wildly successful *2001: A Space Odyssey* (1968) was a major sign that fantastical stories could win viewers and serious critical acclaim; *Star Wars* (1977) caused a decisive commercial shift towards sci-fi and fantasy that has lasted decades since. Lucas and his team invented new technology to make his films, and soon other studios started trying to compete, starting an SFX and VFX arms race that still rages. The result is bigger and more spectacular sci-fi and fantasy films.

The importance of money

Blockbuster hits *The Matrix* (1999) and *The Lord of the Rings* (2001) similarly pushed both genres forward; director Peter Jackson found

Star Wars

George Lucas's series merits particular attention because of the way it changed cinema. Lucas was the first to successfully push to capture the kinetic effects of real-world dogfights in space: where TV's *Star Trek* had imagined starships like ships, he saw them as Spitfires and Hurricanes. He also took his stunts more seriously than his 50s progenitors, bringing in fencing coach Bob Anderson, who had worked with Errol Flynn, to polish his duels. After the staginess and static sets of 1950s efforts like *Forbidden Planet* (1956), this felt miraculous. Over the course of two sequels, numerous spin-offs and three prequels before he handed over the keys to the kingdom, Lucas's space operas opened endless doors for sci-fi and fantasy filmmaking.

himself in a position post-*Rings* akin to Lucas post-*Star Wars*, making more big-budget, fantastical movies to feed the production machine he had built and keep his team employed. Similarly, the ten-year production run of *Harry Potter* films allowed the creation and nurturing of a VFX industry in the United Kingdom that became world-leading. But there was also a clear appetite from audiences, with sci-fi and fantasy films consistently and overwhelmingly dominating the box office for the entire 21st century to date. Low-budget sci-fi and fantasy also made an impact however: the micro-budgeted time travel effort *Safety Not Guaranteed* (2012) launched Colin Trevorrow's career, while Jonathan Glazer's *Under The Skin* (2013) took a distinctly elliptical look at alien invasion.

For much of the 20th century, the sheer expense of live-action fantasy and sci-fi filmmaking meant that it was a primarily American effort, out of reach for the cinema of all but the biggest markets. There were exceptions, like Toho's Godzilla films but, unless you define fantasy as anything at all with any supernatural or mythological element, not many of them. However, digital technology and burgeoning ambition has led to an explosion in both genres worldwide in recent decades. Huge recent hits like *The Mermaid* (2016) from China and *RRR* (2022) from India have been exported successfully around the world, while even the low-budget films of Nigeria have engaged significantly with supernatural and fantastical themes.

Fantasy's slow start

It is probably fair to note that fantasy still lags behind science fiction in onscreen portrayals. Unless you draw the parameters of the genre broadly to include all monster movies and ghost stories – something that is arguable but feels inexact – it was underrepresented between the end of the silent era and the start of the 1980s (*Krull*; 1983 and *Legend*; 1985). However, while there were some likeable and lasting fantasies from that era, such as *Labyrinth* (1986) and *Willow* (1988), most still suffered shonky effects and underwhelming impact. It was not until photo-real, computer-assisted VFX arrived in the mid-1990s that the calculus for fantasy changed, helped hugely by Jackson's *Rings* trilogy. After that, the early 2000s franchises of Warner Bros' *Harry Potter* and Disney's *Pirates of the Caribbean* established fantasy as a box-office heavy-hitter, and if it still lacks the auteur-driven cachet of some sci-fi, it has at least become a reliable fixture in the release calendar.

These genres' flights of imagination allow cinema to reach its full potential, showing us sights that we cannot see in reality. They are immersive to a far greater degree than theatre or literature for many people, and require none of the expertise of gaming. Some fans of James Cameron's *Avatar* in 2009 reported feeling depressed that they could not literally visit his imagined planet of Pandora, so complete was their immersion in its world. Sci-fi and fantasy bring us bizarre creatures with human levels of feeling and emotion, in places that do not exist, and can smuggle in philosophical ideas and social or political commentary as well as space battles – at least, when the executives handling their huge budgets allow it. That is not only something that is valuable for children.

The condensed idea
Endless visual creativity and storytelling daring

Glossary

4K definition A digital image that is approximately (different standards exist) four thousand pixels across.

Arthouse A film made for artistic reasons and a niche audience rather than with wide commercial or popular appeal in mind.

Backlighting The practice of lighting the background of a shot, or casting light on an actor from behind.

Blaxploitation An African American cinema movement of the early 1970s, marrying heightened thriller and action storylines with Black characters and communities.

Block book A classic Hollywood practice whereby studios booked cinemas without theatre owners knowing or controlling what films they would be asked to show.

Chiaroscuro A term in Renaissance art used to describe the use of strong contrasts between light and dark, now used in film and contemporary art.

Cineaste Originally from the French, where it refers to a filmmaker, in English this usually refers to a film lover or student of film.

Clean-ups A practice of doing small, VFX adjustments to an image to remove unwanted elements: plane contrails in a period-set story, for example.

Counter-culture The anti-establishment movement of the 1960s that challenged conservative post-World War II ideals, promoted peace and called for greater civil rights.

Department heads Immediately under a director during the making of a film are 'department heads'. They include the production designer, costume designer and director of photography.

Dissolve (n) A filmmaking term where one image fades – or dissolves – into another, which may include two shots overlapping for a few frames.

Entr'acte A theatre term for the music played between two acts, possibly (though not necessarily) during an intermission.

Exit music A theatre term for the music played as an audience leaves the auditorium, which can refer to a film's end credits accompaniment.

Femme fatale A seductive woman who uses her beauty and appeal to manipulate others to her cause, and who creates a moral or physical danger for the men she encounters.

Fourth wall The barrier between the screen and the audience: a character 'breaks' the fourth wall when they address the audience directly.

Green screen A bright green background placed around actors and sets to facilitate the later addition of visual effects. The screen may also be blue.

Heteronormativity The assumption or belief that heterosexual relations between cisgender partners of the opposite sex is 'normal' for humans.

Intermission An interval or break during the screening of a film. It is common only in very long films and in film traditions with longer running times (Indian film, for example).

Intertitle A text card projected during a film. Commonly used in silent films to offer dialogue, they may still be used to establish place or timeframe.

Kuleshov effect A phenomenon using the juxtaposition of images in sequence to communicate emotion or narrative to viewers.

Matte A matte masks part of an image so it can be replaced by another image. This is used to combine, for example, actors and background.

Metatextuality The analysis of a relationship between different texts, or films, in order to elucidate both.

Multiple exposure The exposure of the same cell of film more than once, creating an in-camera blend of film elements.

Newsreel A short documentary form used between the 1910s and 1970s, of particular importance during the world wars.

Non-diegetic sound Sounds added to a film in post-production that do not originate with anything onscreen – a soundtrack, for example.

Overture Music played before a theatrical performance; used occasionally in film to refer to music before the film starts.

Pan A horizontal camera movement along a central axis.

Romcom Shorthand for 'romantic comedy', a blend of the two genres that could tip more towards either of the two.

Screen test An actor's on-camera audition, allowing casting directors to see how their performance looks on film. Also used in the old studio system to decide who to put under a studio contract.

Soft focus A deliberate choice to slightly blur a shot or elements of it, reducing the amount of detail in the image and creating a dreamy or romantic effect.

Steadicam A brand name for a stabilizing camera mount invented by Garrett Brown in 1975 and allowing long, travelling shots without extraneous motion.

Stop-motion animation An animation technique where models are photographed and moved by tiny increments repeatedly, to create the illusion of movement when projected together.

Stop trick A Georges Méliès technique where a camera is paused and something added to, or removed from, a scene, creating the illusion of its sudden appearance or disappearance.

Sweet spot The optimal place in a theatre for perfect 3D images.

Synecdoche A figure of speech where a part of the thing is used to denote the whole of a thing – for example, a 'hired hand' for a worker; 'wheels' for a car.

Technicolor A colour film process named after the company incorporated in 1915 to exploit its use, and the most popular Hollywood colour film between the late 1920s and 1960s.

Two-shot A film shot showing two people in the frame.

Vaudeville An originally French form of theatrical variety entertainment that included musical and comic elements. It was similar to British music hall theatre, and popular in the United States and Canada in the late 19th and early 20th centuries.

Index

180-degree rule 26

4DX 48

Absurdism 109
action movies 188
  action franchises 189–90
  action origins 188–9
  action stars 190–1
  diversity 188
Amores Perros (2000) 138
Anderson, Wes 34
Anger, Kenneth
  Hollywood Babylon 160
Angry Young Men 118
animation 60–1
  animation 'on twos' 53
  anime 63
  computer-generated images (CGI) 62
  development 61–2
Apollinaire, Guillaume 108
Arzner, Dororthy 162
aspect ratios 49–51
auteur theory 148–51
  female filmmakers 150

Bicycle Thieves (1948) 112
Bollywood 12
Bower, Scotty *Full Service* 160
Buñuel, Luis 111

Cameron, James 55
Cardiff, Jack 17
Casablanca (1942) 197
Cinema Novo 133
cinéma vérité 64–5
cinemas 9–11
cinematography 28–9
  cinematography and technology 29–31
  style and collaboration 30–1
close-ups 24–5
  purpose of the close-up 25–6
  uses of the close-up 26–7

Code (Motion Picture Production Code) 80–1
  case for censorship 81
  challenges to the Code 82–3
  Code and race 80
  Code and women 82
colour films 16–18
  colour scepticism 18–19
comedies 192
  cultural differences 194
  farce and ferocity 193–5
  gross out 195
  Laurel and Hardy 192
  slapstick 192–3
computer-generated images (CGI) 45, 62
Coppola, Francis Ford 85
copyright law 10
coverage 25

De Palma, Brian *Creative Screenwriting* 181
del Toro, Guillermo 136
Die Hard (1988) 89
digital cameras 54–5
digital intermediate (DI) 18
direct cinema 64–5
Disney, Walt 60
distribution 68
  development 69–70
  international variation 71
documentaries 64–5
  modern documentaries 65–7
Dogme 144–5
  female filmmakers 147
  purpose of Dogme 145–7

Eastwood, Clint 175
editing 20–1
  continuity editing 21
  types of edit 21–3

Eisenstein, Sergei 153
Expressionism 104
  Expressionism in cinema 104–6
  lasting legacy 107

fantasy 200–1
  importance of money 201–2
  Oscars 202
  slow development 203
feature films 12–13
  early feature-length films 13–15
Fellini, Federico 114
female filmmakers 87, 147, 150, 198
  gaze theory 156–9
film noir 180–1
  femme fatale 182
  psychology and politics of noir 182–3
  what is noir? 181
films 3
  birth of the big screen 88–9
  development of moving images 5–7
  early film industry 9–11
'foley' art (sound effects) 38
Ford, John 173
formats 48
  aspect ratios 49–51
  format development 48–9
  format switching 50
frame rates 52
  digital cameras 54–5
  working with sound 52–3
franchises 96–8
  canon 98
  shared universes 97
French New Wave 116–19
Freud, Sigmund 106

Gabriel, Teshome *Third Cinema Updated* 135
gaze theory 156–7
  developing an oppositional gaze 158

visual pleasure and narrative cinema 157–8
German Expressionism 104–7
Goebbels, Joseph 197–8
Griffith, David Wark 73

Hardy, Oliver 192
Hays Code *see* Code
high concept films 88
  high concept vs the B-movie 88–9
  look, hook and book 89–91
Hollywood 73–4, 84
  New Hollywood 84–7
horror films 176
  first golden age 176–8
  gorno vs elevated horror 178–9
  remakes 178
Huxley, Aldous *The Olive Tree* 196
hyperlink editing 23

I Am Cuba (1964) 30
Indian film 128
  history 128–9
  international acclaim and influence 131
  masala films 129–31
indie films 92–5
  independent breakthroughs 93
  mini major studios 94
intimacy coordinators 102
Italian neorealism 112–15

Japanese cinema 120–3, 155
  J-horror 177
  Westerns 174
John Wick (2014–25) 190

K-horror 177
Khan, Aamir 130
Khan, Salman 130
Khan, Shah Rukh 130

kinetoscope 6
Kurosawa, Akira 121

Lang, Fritz 105
Laurel, Stan 192
leitmotif 37
linguistic film theory 164–5
Linklater, Richard 92
Living in Bondage (1992) 142
Loach, Ken 154
Lubezki, Emmanuel 137

martial arts movies 124
 cinema origins 124–5
 kung-fu movies 125–7
 wuxia 127
Marxist film theory 152–153
 Marxist analysis 153–4
matte painting 47
Menken, Alan 187
#MeToo 100–1
 aftermath 102–3
 why Hollywood? 101–2
Metz, Christian 165
Mexican cinema 136
 disaster and rebirth 136–8
 new horizons 138–9
mise-en-scène 32
 director as architect 35
 framing, lighting and setting the scene 33–5
mockumentaries 67
Monaco, James 166
montage 20–1
Moore, Michael 66
movie stars 56, 59
 box-office draws and box-office poison 58
 first stars 57
 studio stars 56–8
Mulvey, Laura 156–9
mumblecore 146
Murnau, F W 105
musicals 184, 187
 development 184
 gotta dance! 184–6

musical masking 185
 musicals worldwide 186

neorealism 112–15
Nero, Franco 110
New Wave 116–17
 in search of imperfection 118–19
 young Turks 117–18
Newman, Kim *Nightmare Movies* 179
Nigerian film 140–2
no wave cinema 145
Nollywood 141
non-linear editing 23
Nosferatu (1922) 106
Nykvist, Sven 28

Oscars 14, 202
Ozu, Yasujirō 120

Pinteau, Pascal *Special Effects* 40
post-structuralism 166–7
postmodernism 168
 definition of postmodernism 169–70
 postmodernism onscreen 170–1
 pre-postmodernism 168–9
praxinoscope 5
propaganda films 196
 birth of persuasion 196–7
 Goebbels and World War II 197–8
 post-World War II 198–9

queer theory 160–1
 history 161–2
 New Queer Cinema 163

Ray, Satyajit 129
Red Shoes, The (1948) 32
Riefenstahl, Leni 198
Rossellini, Roberto 113
Russo, Vito 162

Sarris, Andrew 148
Schwarzenegger, Arnold 189
science fiction 200–1
 importance of money 201–2
 Oscars 202
scores 38–9
Scorsese, Martin 86
Scream (1996) 170
Sembène, Ousmane 134
Shaw Brothers 126
silent films 72–3
 cinema as art 74–5
 Hollywood triumphant 73–4
slapstick 192–3
Smell-o-Vision 48
Sondheim, Stephen 186
sound 36
 development of sound 36–7
 frame rates 52–3
 sound effects 38
 soundtracks and score 37–8
Soviet montage theory 20
special effects (SFX) 40
 development of SFX 40–2
 visual effects (VFX) 42–3
Spielberg, Steven 90
split screen editing 22
Star Wars 201
streaming 70
structuralist film theory 165–6
 structural films 166
studio system 76
 erosion of the system 79
 film industry 76–8
stunts 42
Surrealism 108–11
Swanson, Gloria 27

Tarantino, Quentin 93, 168
Tarkovsky, Andrei *Sculpting in Time* 33
Technicolor 16–18
tendency films 155

Thalberg, Irving G 78
Third Cinema 132
 definition and practice 132–4
 limitations and decline 134–5
Toho Studios 123
Truffaut, François 117
Trumbull, Douglas 54
two-shots 24

United Artists 77

Varda, Agnès 116
VHS (video home system) 68
Vinterberg, Thomas 144
visual effects (VFX) 42–3, 44
 development 44–5
 going digital 48–51

Warner, Jack L 76
Weinstein, Harvey 100–1
West, Mae 83
Westerns 172
 development 172
 glory days 173–4
 Japanese cinema 174
 revisionism, death and rebirth 174–5
Wilder, Billy 180
Williams, 195
Winston, Stan 41
Woo-ping, Yuen 125
Wood, Evan Rachel 101
Yen, Donnie 124

Zsigmond, Vilmos 29

About the Author

Helen O'Hara is a film journalist,
Editor-at-Large for *Empire* magazine and
co-host of the *Empire* podcast. She is also the
author of five books, including *Women vs Hollywood:
The Fall and Rise of Women in Film*.

First published in Great Britain in 2025 by Greenfinch
An imprint of Quercus Editions Limited
Carmelite House
50 Victoria Embankment
London EC4Y 0DZ

An Hachette UK company

The authorised representative in the EEA is Hachette Ireland, 8 Castlecourt Centre, Dublin 15, D15 XTP3, Ireland (email: info@hbgi.ie)

A CIP catalogue record for this book is available from the British Library

PB ISBN 978-1-52944-396-7
eBook ISBN 978-1-52944-397-4

SRD

Cover design by Luke Bird

Printed and bound in India by Manipal Technologies Limited, Manipal